ENDORSEMENTS

Modern life has produced a new skill called "compartmentaliza-tion". The idea is that our lives are so busy with so many things, one needs to separate the various categories in our minds to survive. Work may be going terribly, but if we compartmentalize it, it won't affect our home life. We may have pressing financial problems, but it needs to be roped off so that the money stress won't ruin all the other areas of our lives.

In his new book, Tom Copland calls that into question. Can life really be broken into separate, disconnected, neatly unrelat-ed pieces? Tom carefully follows the Scriptures and discovers that many of the "compartments" are not separate at all but are instead inextricably linked. Money is connected to our relation-ship with God, our family, and even our eternal reward. Follow Tom as he untangles the modern clutter and presents a holistic, biblical world view that leads to a natural action-oriented plan.

It's true that responding biblically to finances will put some starch in your bank account, but there is something so much more beautiful than a favourable monthly bank statement, such as rewards in heaven. The lives around you will be enriched and your ministry will be deepened as you apply what Tom teaches in this book. I commend it to you!

Rev. Don Symons, senior pastor Westney Heights Baptist Church, Ajax, Ontario, Canada; former executive with a large multinational technology company

Management of Money Impacts Relationship with God, Spouse, and Eternity is a very impactful and sobering read that turns the focus from the practical benefits of managing God's resources

His way (as presented within *Financial Moments, Biblical Principles that Will Transform How You Manage Money*, and *Debt Reduction: Biblical Principles to Deal with Inflation, High Interest Rates, and Eliminating Debt*) to the spiritual benefits from doing so. I have studied Tom's core material on financial management God's way within various formats over the last several years, and the teaching and exhortation within this book provide a fresh perspective on how our actual day-to-day choices can affect us for all eternity. I recommend this material for everyone as a tool that can help the reader reflect on how the tangible (yet finite) resources gifted to us from the Lord (time and money) can connect to the meaning and purpose of our lives, which He has ultimately called us to.

Eli Papakirykos, Chartered Financial Analyst

I found Tom's book, *Management of Money Impacts Relationship with God, Spouse, and Eternity*, an excellent read and extremely helpful. I literally had to stop while reading it to thank God for Tom, for how he so thoroughly presented what the Scriptures teach regarding the correlation between money and how it impacts all our relationships—with God, spouse, family, and friends. In this book, Tom presents scriptural truth relating to money that I've never heard before. It was so simply and yet so profound. I sincerely believe everyone should read this book. You will find it to be an excellent guide for every area of your life, as it relates to our time now as well as from an eternal perspective; especially as it relates to the finances God has entrusted to us.

Randy Ziegenhagel, financial coach and culture development adviser, former global culture officer and VP of business development and electronics manufacturing industry

God has entrusted Tom with a mandate of great consequence: to study and teach financial biblical truths that run counter to the cultural and social narrative. In this book, Tom challenges the reader to consider a paradigm shift—from managing our money, time, and talents from a temporal perspective to an eternal one. This sentiment is grounded in faith and emphasizes an overarching principle in the Bible: beyond how we live our lives today and during our time on earth, we must consider the implications of our actions on how we will spend eternity.

Anthony Martino, MBA, Chartered Professional Accountant

I have known Tom Copland for over 25 years. While I was the Canadian Director for InTouch Ministries, Tom ran financial seminars for our donor base, and I can testify that he was a blessing to hundreds of people. I can highly recommend his book because it is totally based on Scripture.

Art Brooker, chairman of the board, Intouch Ministries of Canada

Tom repeats and expands on many financial principles … repetition is good. Except for the case studies, this is a workbook, not a light read. It is not "prosperity gospel" stuff, but he certainly speaks of eternal rewards and benefits of wise financial stewardship decisions now.

Rev. Jack Hannah, retired pastor, having ministered for over five decades

Tom's deep understanding and many years of experience provide a wealth of knowledge for readers. He clearly shows how knowing and implementing God's financial principles impact our everyday lives and relationships, as well as having impacts in eternity. It is both thought-provoking and practical. A book that is beneficial for everyone to read and apply.

Rebekah Young, financial coach

In *Management of Money Impacts Relationship with God, Spouse, and Eternity*, Tom provides practical insights on how managing money impacts relationships, eternity, and our testimony for the Lord. With solid biblical references and compelling anecdotes, this thought-provoking book challenges readers to examine their perspectives on money and make wise decisions that honour God. From practical tips on managing money in marriage and parenting to shifting focus from earthly treasures to treasures in heaven, this book offers invaluable guidance. I highly recommend *Money Matters* to anyone seeking a biblical perspective on financial management.

Dan Tomlinson, MBA, BASc Engineering, financial coach and small group leader of Financial Management God's Way

TESTIMONIES

Dear Tom, I attended one of your courses many years ago. Your teaching and your humbleness before the Lord have stayed with me. Thanks be to God I am debt-free and I'm able to be used to help others in this world. Many, many thanks for your ministry.

L.P. from Toronto, Canada

Hallelujah! Knowing the state of your flocks will save you money. May God be praised! Thank you for your financial seminar for singles I took last year. Your seminars are excellent biblical teaching that works, and I am still using it today. Thank you, Tom, and thank you, God!

P.H. from Vancouver, Canada

As a result of the seminar, I actually paid off all my credit cards and two lines of credit. I realized that I had a good job and could pay them off but constantly was spending my income, so I consciously started sending my extra pay and targeting those credit sources and got out of debt there. Now I just have to focus on paying off my mortgage. Thank you for your help.

C.E., Oakville, Ontario

Your ministry is a blessing to me and my family. I am very appreciative of your "all wise" emails.

D.M. and C.B., Nova Scotia Canada

Tom you are without a doubt one of the most humble people I have ever had the privilege to listen to. That has to be the reason why the Holy Spirit draws so many people to your teachings, He is your partner … God Bless.

D.W.P., Shawville, Québec, Canada

I am doing your four-part financial online course. I am so blessed to be a part of this course. My financial situation is a burden to me, and I am so encouraged by these sessions. I saw you on TV about a year ago and have been blessed since. Praying the Lord will continue to bless you abundantly as you help us with our financial situation so that we can have peace and joy as children of God.

D.S., Brampton, Ontario

I really like how finances are part of the Bible and how this is taught so very well at Copland Financial Ministries. And the fact that Christ is the center of the teachings is truly noteworthy! I tell many of my friends about your ministry in order to show them so they can experience peace when they and we are all doing everything through Christ. Thank you so much; blessings on your ministry!

E.K., Calgary, Alberta, Canada

In my walk of over twenty years, I have never heard such a wonderful ministry as yours. It is so refreshing and unique to hear the Bible related to finances. It is such a touchy subject that I believe we as Christians try to avoid it and just blindly give our money. When we should be listening to the Spirit prompting us to promote the Kingdom of God and be true stewards of His money. May God bless your ministry!

G.S., Dartmouth, Nova Scotia, Canada

The key difference for me has been a renewing of my mind. I am more focused on my stewardship of not just God's money but also my time and other resources He has blessed me with … I am becoming more aware of spending choices, such as impulse buying and giving no matter how worthy that may seem. My purchases are more considered and I am definitely saving intentionally based on the Tom Copland Budgeting System. Thank you!

A.A.W., Hertfordshire, United Kingdom

I have been following your messages for several years because I truly believe that God is speaking to us through you. Your words of wisdom are required today in the midst of the confusion and commotion created by the media. Thank you so much, and may the Lord continue to bless you and your loved ones and give you good health and long life to carry on this wonderful mission.

Tino, Cebu, Philippines

Hi, Tom. Thank you so much for what you do. You are literally the only person I have ever found in Canada who explains how to deal in a biblical way with our financial messes we've made.

T.M., Wasaga, Ontario, Canada

Thank you so much, Tom. These teachings have been invaluable to me. I have started the eight-part series for young people, and it is proving to be revolutionary. I very much appreciate the free material and your willingness to help me become financially smarter. I am really grateful!

J.A., Brampton, Ontario, Canada

I've been an adult for several decades and have committed to monthly giving for my charities and church. I had no idea, before taking this course, that God was so "invested" in the topic of finances. As I read my Bible now, I notice references to money and regard them as actual financial advice and not just metaphors using money. The budgeting material (in particular) has been very helpful. Thank you. I'm grateful to have had the opportunity to take this course. Thank you, Tom, for your ministry.

B.B., Edmonton, Alberta, Canada

MANAGEMENT OF MONEY IMPACTS

RELATIONSHIP WITH GOD, SPOUSE, AND ETERNITY

WITH TOM COPLAND
(Chartered Professional Accountant)

Published by Castle Quay Books
Burlington, Ontario, Canada and Jupiter, Florida, U.S.A.
416-573-3249 | info@castlequaybooks.com | www.castlequaybooks.com

Edited by Julie Child
Cover design and book interior by Burst Impressions

978-1-988928-92-0 Soft Cover
978-1-988928-93-7 E-book

Library and Archives Canada Cataloguing in Publication
Title: Management of money impacts relationship with God, spouse and eternity / by Tom Copland.
Names: Copland, Tom, 1953- author.
Description: Includes bibliographical references.
Identifiers: Canadiana 20230471730 | ISBN 9781988928920 (softcover)
Subjects: LCSH: Money—Biblical teaching. | LCSH: Finance, Personal—Biblical teaching.
Classification: LCC BS680.M57 C65 2023 | DDC 220.8/332024—dc23

CASTLE QUAY BOOKS

I dedicate this book to my Saviour and Lord, Jesus Christ, who has created me with the passion and ability to teach His word on finances.

My prayer is to continue to serve Him diligently and faithfully for the rest of my life. "For God's gifts and his call are irrevocable" (Romans 11:29).

The NIRV translation puts it this way, "God does not take back his gifts. He does not change his mind about those he has chosen."

CONTENTS

ABOUT THE AUTHOR

Tom Copland has been teaching God's word on finances since 1982 as a faithful servant of the Lord Jesus Christ.

Throughout the years, Tom has been privileged to help thousands of people learn and apply God's way of managing money. Further, his teaching ministry and biblically-based financial counseling have helped countless individuals and couples achieve complete freedom from debt!

As part of his "Financial Moments" series, Tom condenses biblical financial principles into one-minute summaries. Currently, 386 "Financial Moments" are broadcast on 193 radio stations and seven television stations across Canada and the northern United States. According to estimates, approximately 2.3 million people listen to at least one "Financial Moment" weekly. Further, Tom has recorded nearly 100 half-hour programs broadcast across 52 radio stations and seven television stations in Canada and the northern United States.

In addition, Tom has authored several books, including *Financial Management God's Way*, an in-depth study that teaches money management according to biblical principles. Some topics covered are how to get out of debt, a worldly versus a biblical understanding of money, budgeting, obtaining godly counsel, giving generously, investing, financial deceptions, stewardship, and comparison of a secular versus a biblical perspective on money.

Tom's most recent book, *Debt Reduction: Biblical Principles to Deal with Inflation, High Interest Rates, and Eliminating Debt*, is an excellent read that addresses the major financial concerns most people are dealing with because of high interest rates and inflation.

Lastly, as a Chartered Professional Accountant, Tom owns and operates a public accounting firm in Markham, Ontario, Canada, which provides biblically-based financial advice in conjunction with its corporate accounting and tax services. The business website is www.copland-ca.com.

ACKNOWLEDGEMENTS

I want to thank Henry Enriquez, my tech support, who has devoted over 26 years of his time and expertise to help me with my ministry, performing many tasks too numerous to mention. I very much appreciate his faithful support and dedication over the years.

I extend my gratitude to Art Brooker, the chairman of the board of In Touch Ministries of Canada, for the idea of the "Financial Moments" series. I am also thankful to Art for connecting me with the right individuals in radio and television to make the expansion of this vital ministry possible.

Additionally, I would like to thank Pastor Don Symons and Pastor Jack Hannah, the two pastors of my church, for being pillars of support, both personally and for the ministry to which God has called me. I sincerely thank Pastor Don Symons for his collaboration on the teaching series "Dealing with Inflation and High Interest Rates from a Biblical Perspective," now available on our website at www.coplandfinancialministries.org.

Moreover, I would like to thank my dear friend, Cam Golberg, who has been a tremendous help and an outstanding small group leader of the "Financial Management God's Way" series.

I am also grateful for the dedicated financial coaches and small group leaders who have volunteered to teach hundreds how to manage money biblically through the "Financial Management God's Way" sessions. These leaders include Anthony Martino, Dan Tomlinson, Eli Papakirykos, Christine Kewallal, Liisa Snell, Randy Ziegenhagel, and Efrain Soto—who also translated a significant portion of my in-depth biblical financial study into Spanish.

Finally, I would like to thank Julie Child for her excellent editing work and Castle Quay Books for publishing this book in recognition of my vision.

MY PERSONAL TESTIMONY

Since 1982, the Lord gave me a clear revelation of what He created me to do with my earthly life. It is my heart's desire to share how God called me to teach His word on finances. Psalm 139:13–16 states:

> "For you created my inmost being;
>   you knit me together in my mother's womb.
>
> I praise you because I am fearfully and wonderfully made;
>   your works are wonderful,
>   I know that full well.
>
> My frame was not hidden from you
>   when I was made in the secret place,
>   when I was woven together in the depths of the earth.
>
> Your eyes saw my unformed body;
>   all the days ordained for me were written in your book
>   before one of them came to be."

Thus, when God created me in my mother's womb, He specifically planned and purposed for me to teach His word on finances. It's not a coincidence that I became a chartered accountant before I even came to know the Lord! Then, shortly after I accepted Jesus Christ as my Saviour and Lord on April 12, 1981, God revealed that His calling for my life was to teach and advise others how to manage the money entrusted to them according to biblical principles.

I remain steadfast in my commitment to serving the Lord faithfully and wholeheartedly throughout my life for His ultimate glory. My goal is to please my heavenly Father, help others, and "finish well" before I enter eternity. I consider myself a humble servant of the Lord Jesus Christ, as my gift to teach comes from Him, not from me, for He is the one who made me and equipped me to do what He has called me to do. Romans 11:29 states, "For God's gifts and his call are irrevocable." Therefore, I am God's servant, created and called to teach His word on finances—a calling I will carry for the rest of my life, one the Lord will never remove from me!

As a result, it is vital for me to teach Christians how to manage their money, material possessions, time, and talents, so their lives will be significantly impacted on earth and for eternity!

The purpose of this book, then, is to help people understand that how they manage money and resources will directly impact their relationship with God, their spouse, others, and eternity.

INTRODUCTION

As of March 2023, while writing this book, interest rates in Canada, the United States, and worldwide have risen faster than any other one-year period in history! Equally alarming is that inflation reached a 40-year high by the summer of 2022, and it remains a major problem today.

Since most people carry significant debt, the rise in interest rates has profoundly hurt many of them. Since variable interest rates have quadrupled over the last year, some homeowners saw their mortgage payments and personal credit lines increase by 50 to 80 per cent. Increased interest rates combined with a substantial rise in the cost of living have resulted in tremendous financial hardships for many individuals and couples.

However, it doesn't matter how much money you owe. Remember that we serve the King of kings and the Lord of lords—the God of the universe who created *everything* in six days! As such, He is more than able to help you pay your bills and overcome debt if you learn to manage money according to His biblical financial principles and His specific direction for your life. In Psalm 32:8, the Lord says, "I will instruct you and teach you in the way you should go; I will counsel you with my loving eye on you."

As an accountant and financial adviser, I've seen thousands of people with so much debt they believed their situation was hopeless. Yet, once they committed to managing money God's way, God's hand began to move! The Lord helped them reduce their debt and meet their financial obligations on time, sometimes through miraculous interventions!

In addition, I've seen debt accumulation combined with higher interest rates result in tensions between husbands and wives, often destroying their marriage relationship. And almost without exception, they were in financial trouble because they violated God's financial principles, often unknowingly.

However, couples who have learned and applied biblical financial principles were able to pay down debt and get their finances under control. I've also witnessed many relationships healed and restored when financial pressures eased, resulting in a renewed love for one another! I will discuss how money management impacts a marriage relationship in chapter II of this book.

Randy Alcorn and R.G. LeTourneau said, "You can't take it with you, but you can send it on ahead." Further, a well-known missionary, Jim Elliot, once said, "He is no fool who gives up what he cannot keep to gain what he cannot lose."

In other cases, many people have tried to solve their financial problems by restructuring their debt several times over a few years. But, sadly, this only treats the symptom, not the underlying problem. The problem is that they spend more than they earn and accumulate debt, which God warns against in Proverbs 22:7.

Over the last year, I've received numerous emails and comments from people who have thanked my financial coaches and me for the biblically-based financial advice we gave them. Unlike most people, they have little or no debt, so they are not concerned about higher interest rates. They also have some savings (Proverbs 21:20), so they can handle the increased cost of living. This is consistent with what Jesus taught in the parable of the wise and foolish builders, where He said:

"Therefore everyone who hears these words of mine and puts them into practice is like a wise man who built his house on the rock. The rain came down, the streams rose, and the winds blew and beat against that house; yet it did not fall, because it had its foundation on the rock" (Matthew 7:24–25).

In other words, people who follow God's financial principles will survive these tough times quite easily. However, those who have not managed money God's way will suffer due to higher interest rates and inflation. Note how Jesus confirms this in Matthew 7:26–27:

"Everyone who hears these words of mine and does not put them into practice is like a foolish man who built his house on sand. The rain came down, the streams rose, and the winds blew and beat against that house, and it fell with a great crash."

Interestingly, this parable relates to a "house falling with a great crash." Unfortunately, because of higher interest rates in particular and, to some extent, the increased cost of living, many people will likely lose their homes over the next few years. I'm concerned for these people, and I want to help them.

Another thing most Christians don't realize is that how they manage money can impact their relationship with God, negatively impacting their spiritual growth as they focus on their financial problems and related stress instead of on things of eternal value. In Colossians 3:1–2, the apostle Paul said, "Since, then, you have been raised with Christ, set your hearts on things above, where Christ is seated at the right hand of God. Set your mind on things above, not on earthly things." I discuss this in chapter I.

Further, most Christians are unaware that how they manage their money and material resources, as well as their time and talents God entrusted to them while on earth, will result in rewards or lack of rewards when they stand before the Lord at the "judgment seat of Christ" (2 Corinthians 5:10), which I cover in detail in chapter VII.

I have used numerous real-life case studies from the past four decades to help you understand the practical application of biblical financial principles. Because God's word contains extensive wisdom concerning money management, I quote many verses from the Bible. Christians are usually comfortable with this. However, *even if you're not a Christian*, I encourage you to read this book. I know from experience that you will benefit significantly in the long run if you learn and apply these biblical financial principles.

While reading this book, I encourage you to pray and ask God to speak to your heart and mind by His Holy Spirit, as God can highlight Scriptures to you. For example, Psalm 119:105 says, "Your word is a lamp to my feet and a light to my path" (ESV). God can also give you His peace (John 14:27) or lack of peace concerning any financial decision.

Finally, the Lord has promised to direct us. In Isaiah 48:17, God said, "I am the LORD your God, who teaches you what is best for you, who directs you in the way you should go."

May the Lord bless you and direct you on your personal journey into a deeper understanding of God's word concerning managing the money and material resources He has entrusted to you (Matthew 25:14–30).

Tom Copland, a fellow servant in the Lord Jesus Christ.

I.

MANAGEMENT OF MONEY IMPACTS YOUR RELATIONSHIP WITH GOD

A. OBJECTIVE OF THIS CHAPTER

1. To understand how our handling of money and material things affects our relationship with God and how our relationship with God affects our handling of money and material things.

2. To identify actions and attitudes regarding money that could either hinder or draw us into a closer relationship with the Lord.

B. KEY BIBLICAL PRINCIPLE

How we handle money impacts our relationship with God, and our relationship with God impacts how we manage money. In Luke 16:11, Jesus said, "If you have not been trustworthy in handling worldly wealth, who will trust you with true riches?"

Christians commonly believe there is no connection between their spirituality and how they manage money and possessions. However, in the above verse, Jesus Christ is clear that our faithful stewardship of money (or lack thereof) will significantly impact the extent to which God entrusts us with His "true riches."

1. What are God's "True Riches"?

What do you think God's true riches are? Please write your thoughts before reading Tom's comments.

_____

_____

_____

TOM'S COMMENT

God's "true riches" are things that are imperishable and extremely important to God. They originate from God and include the following:

1. *A Close Personal Relationship with God:* Our relationship with God through His Son, Jesus Christ, is the most important thing in life. According to the apostle Paul, our relationship with Christ is more valuable than anything else (Philippians 3:8).

2. *God's Peace:* God promises us His peace when we allow Him to direct us by His Spirit. "The mind governed by the flesh is death, but the mind governed by the Spirit is life and peace" (Romans 8:6).

3. *God's Joy:* God promises us His joy when we are in His presence. Psalm 16:11 states, "In Your presence is fullness of joy" (NKJV).

2. Management of Money Impacts our Relationship with God

At first, it may be difficult to believe that our faithful stewardship of money (or lack thereof) will affect our relationship with God and the joy and peace He gives. However, money can be a serious competitor in our relationship with God, which Jesus made clear in Matthew 6:24:

> "No one can serve two masters. Either you will hate the one and love the other, or you will be devoted to the one and despise the other. You cannot serve both God and money."

Let's look at a typical example of how money management can impact our relationship with God: If an individual or couple spends more than they earn regularly, they will experience financial difficulties in due course.

Generally speaking, financially stressed people spend much time and energy focused on their financial problems.

As a result, their relationship with God is inadvertently impacted. In Matthew 6:21, Jesus said, "For where your treasure is, there your heart will be also." If money-related problems dominate our hearts, how can we be free to love God with all our heart, soul, strength, and mind? (See Luke 10:27.)

Consequently, the anxiety that comes from financial problems and excessive debt usually results in a lack of peace and joy in one's life. Have you ever met anyone who was happy to miss a mortgage installment or car loan payment?

Another example is a Christian with a compelling desire for money and material things, as even Christians can struggle with the love of money, negatively impacting their relationship with the Lord. First Timothy 6:10 reminds us, "The *love of money* is a root of all kinds of evil. Some people, eager for money, have wandered from the faith and pierced themselves with many griefs" (emphasis added).

Please note that "the love of money" is a root of all kinds of evil, not money in and of itself. Some characteristics of ungodly attitudes towards money and material things include selfishness, greed, pride, covetousness, materialism, lack of contentment, obsession with riches, and living beyond one's means.

On the other hand, a Christian who manages money in a godly fashion—being content with God's provision and living within the means provided by God—will experience God's "true riches" such as an intimate relationship with the Lord, and God's peace and joy.

The following illustrates other ways our management of money and possessions impact our relationship with God.

3. Our Relationship with God Impacts How We Manage Money

Do you believe a person's relationship with God impacts how they manage money? Prayerfully consider your answer with a reference to Scripture before viewing Tom's comments.

_____

_____

_____

TOM'S COMMENT

Christians who have a close personal relationship with Jesus Christ seek biblical wisdom in all areas of life. Further, they manage their money and resources in a godly fashion dependent upon God.

As a result, they characteristically do the following:

1. They seek and obtain God's wisdom (James 1:5) in managing the money He entrusts to them (1 Corinthians 4:2).

2. They renew their minds (Romans 12:2) by regularly meditating on God's word (Joshua 1:8). In doing so, they understand and apply biblical financial principles in managing money.

3. They follow God's financial principles (Psalm 111:10), thereby avoiding many financial difficulties that even followers of Christ may encounter if they willfully or unknowingly violate biblical principles.

4. They hear God's voice and follow His specific will for their lives (John 10:27).

5. They give God the "first fruits" of their income (Proverbs 3:9), and God blesses them (Proverbs 3:10).

6. They have minimal or no debt (Proverbs 22:7) and avoid pressure from creditors and lenders, which *can be a tremendous distraction from their relationship with the Lord and any ministry endeavours.*

7. They follow Jesus Christ's admonition to plan ahead and develop and implement a budget or spending plan (see the parable of the tower in Luke 14:28–30).

8. They track their expenses to know where their money is going—to know their "financial facts" rather than making financial decisions based on guesswork or personal desires (Proverbs 27:23).

9. They obtain financial counsel from God (1 Kings 22:5), God's word (Psalm 119:24), and godly financial advisers (1 Corinthians 2:14–15).

10. Finally, they are content with God's provision thereby avoiding ungodly attitudes of covetousness, selfishness, pride and greed, leading to many financial problems (1 Timothy 6:6–8).

C. SCRIPTURE VERSES RELATED TO UNGODLY ATTITUDES TOWARD MONEY

God's word provides serious warnings against ungodly attitudes, as seen in the following Scriptures:

"You shall not covet your neighbor's house. You shall not covet your neighbor's wife, or his male or female servant, his ox or donkey, or anything that belongs to your neighbor" (Exodus 20:17).

"Do nothing out of selfish ambition or vain conceit. Rather, in humility value others above yourselves, not looking to your own interests but each of you to the interests of others" (Philippians 2:3–4).

Likewise, in Luke 12:15, Jesus warned, "Watch out! Be on your guard against all kinds of greed; life does not consist in an abundance of possessions."

In summary, believers who enjoy a close personal relationship with Jesus Christ will consistently pray and seek God's word for guidance and direction in all areas of life, including managing finances. Therefore, they will manage money and material things in a godly manner with godly attitudes.

As a result, such believers are bound to experience God's peace and joy in financial matters. But, unfortunately, few experience God's peace in their finances as they have not learned and implemented the biblical financial principles in managing the money God has entrusted to them (1 Corinthians 4:2).

D. MEMORY VERSES

There is no substitute for meditating on God's word (Joshua 1:8). To help change how you think about and manage money (Romans 12:2), I encourage you to meditate regularly on the following verses:

"If you have not been trustworthy in handling worldly wealth, who will trust you with true riches?" (Luke 16:11).

"No one can serve two masters. Either you will hate the one and love the other, or you will be devoted to the one and despise the other. You cannot serve both God and money" (Matthew 6:24).

E. CASE STUDIES, QUESTIONS, TOM'S COMMENTS

1. Case Study #1: A Married Couple Keeps Upgrading Their Home

Mark and Sue have been married for 20 years and have two children. Mark earns an average income, and Sue works part-time. Throughout their marriage, they have lived in four houses, each for approximately four years.

With every move, they purchase a larger and nicer home. When they bought their last house, they thought they had found "the one" that would make them happy and meet their needs until retirement. However, they are dissatisfied within two years and desire a bigger, more luxurious house.

Mark and Sue put a lot of time and effort into making their home as beautiful as possible. In the meantime, they keep an eye out for a better house at a reasonable price because they believe upgrading is a smart investment in a rising real estate market.

Moreover, they notice that some of their friends have much nicer homes. As Christians, they believe God wants to bless them abundantly and provide them with a home equivalent to their friends' despite Mark's average income. Unfortunately, their mortgage increases significantly every time they move, leaving them deeply in debt.

As a result, Mark and Sue suffer grievous consequences due to their worldly mindset concerning money and material things, resulting in poor financial decisions. Sadly, Sue has to work full-time *to service their debt,* leaving her less time to spend with her husband, their children, and the Lord.

Further, the couple believes they can no longer afford to tithe. With most of their time and energy focused on improving their home and servicing their debt, Mark and Sue rarely read God's word, pray, or have "quiet time" with the Lord. Their church involvement is also compromised by a lack of time. They reason that as soon as they have less financial stress, they can commit more time to God and their church.

Here are some questions to consider. Before reading my comments, consider your answers and write your suggested solutions in the space provided. Please provide a relevant Scripture reference where able.

QUESTION #1

How would you describe Mark and Sue's attitude with respect to money and material things?

_____

_____

_____

TOM'S COMMENT

Mark and Sue demonstrate several *ungodly, worldly attitudes,* such as:

- They have a problem with covetousness as they are not content with what they have and desire what others have (Exodus 20:17).

- Their lifestyle demonstrates a *love of money and material things* (Hebrews 13:5; 1 Timothy 6:6–8).

- Their priorities are wrong since their home is more important to them than their relationship with God, their children, or other believers.

- They serve a material thing—their home instead of God, which is idolatrous (Matthew 6:24).

QUESTION #2

Do you think Mark and Sue's intense desire to find the "right home" has negatively impacted their relationship with God?

_____

_____

_____

TOM'S COMMENT

Yes, absolutely. Mark and Sue spend too much time and energy renovating their home while trying to find the ideal house. Consequently, their time with the Lord is severely restricted, and they no longer read His word or actively participate in their local church. As a result, their spiritual life and personal relationship with God suffer greatly.

QUESTION #3

As noted, Mark and Sue often take notice of what others have and strongly desire to have at least the equivalent. What does this represent?

TOM'S COMMENT

Mark and Sue have a problem with covetousness (Exodus 20:17), lack of contentment (Hebrews 13:5), selfishness (Philippians 2:3–4), and likely greed (Luke 12:15).

QUESTION #4

Do you believe Mark and Sue's distant relationship with the Lord has affected how they manage money? Please explain.

_____
_____
_____

TOM'S COMMENT

Yes, most certainly, because Mark and Sue's lack of intimacy with the Lord led them to develop worldly attitudes concerning money and material things. As a result, the "ways of the world" have impacted them more than God or His word.

QUESTION #5

In what ways could Mark and Sue's children be affected? What could they inadvertently learn from Mark and Sue's poor example?

_____
_____
_____

TOM'S COMMENT

There is a high risk that Mark and Sue may unintentionally pass on their ungodly and worldly views on money and material things to their children as they are not good financial role models. Consequently, their children are likely to believe the lie (from the world and Satan) that only money and possessions, such as the perfect house, will bring them happiness.

As a result, they may adopt ungodly attitudes like covetousness, selfishness, and greed, which will negatively affect their relationship with the Lord (Matthew 6:24). Further, Mark and Sue's worldly perspective on money and material things could be unintentionally passed down to future generations of grandchildren, great-grandchildren, and so on (Deuteronomy 5:9).

QUESTION #6

What significant challenges could one of their children encounter, assuming they have a modest income and feel led by the Lord to go into full-time ministry?

_____

_____

_____

TOM'S COMMENT

From my experience, Mark and Sue's children will probably adopt similar ungodly and worldly attitudes toward money and material things. As a result, they may end up frustrated and unhappy in full-time ministry because their income would be insufficient to satisfy their material wants and desires. As the saying goes, "It is easy to go up but hard to go down."

Additionally, there is a high risk their children will incur significant debt trying to maintain the standard of living they were accustomed to, growing up. It is also likely they would not follow God's call to full-time ministry if they believed the lie that money and material things bring happiness, which is one "financial deception" Mark and Sue believed.

2. Scripture Application #1

Discuss the relevance and application of the following verses with respect to Mark and Sue's situation. Then, write your comments.

"You shall not covet your neighbor's house. You shall not covet your neighbor's wife, or his male or female servant, his ox or donkey, or anything that belongs to your neighbor" (Exodus 20:17).

_____

_____

_____

_____

_____

_____

TOM'S COMMENT

One of God's commandments is *not to covet* what others have. Mark and Sue have a serious problem with covetousness and need to learn to *be content with God's provision*. Even the apostle Paul, though he was a deeply committed Christian, had to learn to be content. Here's what Paul said in Philippians 4:11–13:

"I am not saying this because I am in need, for I have learned to be content whatever the circumstances. I know what it is to be in need, and I know what it is to have plenty. I have learned the secret of being content in any and every situation, whether well fed or hungry, whether living in plenty or in want. I can do all this through him who gives me strength.

"Keep your lives free from the love of money and be content with what you have, because God has said,
'Never will I leave you;
never will I forsake you'" (Hebrews 13:5).

_____

_____

_____

TOM'S COMMENT

God commands us to be free from the love of money (including material things such as a house) and to be content with His provision. However, it is clear that Mark and Sue have a significant problem with the love of money and material things. Therefore, they must repent and renounce this ungodly attitude with the help of God's wisdom, guidance, and strength (1 Timothy 6:6–8; Philippians 4:11–13).

"Do not store up for yourselves treasures on earth, where moths and vermin destroy, and where thieves break in and steal. But store up for yourselves treasures in heaven, where moths and vermin do not destroy, and where thieves do not break in and steal. For where your treasure is, there your heart will be also" (Matthew 6:19–21).

_____

_____

_____

TOM'S COMMENT

Mark and Sue's efforts to obtain a more lavish home merely store up treasures on earth, which are fleeting and temporary. They need to learn that only treasures in heaven will last for eternity.

Therefore, it would be wise for Mark and Sue to focus their time and energy on treasures in heaven that have eternal value, such as their relationship with God, the salvation of others, and the rewards God gives for faithful service while we are on earth.

"Since, then, you have been raised with Christ, set your hearts on things above, where Christ is, seated at the right hand of God. Set your minds on things above, not on earthly things" (Colossians 3:1–2).

What do you think has been the primary focus of Mark and Sue's hearts?

_____

_____

_____

TOM'S COMMENT

Mark and Sue focus on "treasures on earth," such as their home, and not treasures in heaven that will last for eternity (Matthew 6:19–21; Colossians 3:1–2).

3. Case Study #2: A Couple Struggles with Materialism

Angelo and Maria have been married for 14 years and have two children. Angelo owns and manages a successful business that requires a substantial amount of time, averaging 65 hours per week. As the primary provider for his family, he believes his time commitment to the company is appropriate, while Maria helps out part-time.

The couple owns a large home in Toronto, a cottage in Muskoka, and a Florida condominium. Angelo's high income makes their debt load quite manageable. However, he admits that his biggest struggle is not with his cash flow but with the allocation of his time. Angelo feels strongly that he and his wife must spend a reasonable amount of time at their cottage and Florida condo to be good stewards. In addition, both properties require regular care and maintenance, including servicing their boat and Sea-Doo.

As a Christian, Angelo understands the importance of having quiet devotional time with the Lord, but because of other obligations, he rarely reads God's word or prays. Additionally, he spends little time with his children and lacks time for church involvement. Maria enjoys the prestige that comes with owning all these assets and delights being the envy of her friends. As a busy wife and mother, she also spends limited time cultivating her relationship with the Lord.

QUESTION #1

How would you describe Angelo and Maria's attitude concerning money and material things? Please provide a reference to Scripture.

_____

_____

_____

TOM'S COMMENT

Angelo and Maria have a materialistic and worldly mindset as they struggle with the love of money and material things. By their lifestyle, it is apparent the things of this world are more important to them than their relationship with God, each other, or their children.

Furthermore, they do not make time to fellowship with other believers or serve at their local church, which is contrary to God's word (Hebrews 10:25).

QUESTION #2

Have Angelo and Maria's financial management and attitudes toward money and material things affected their relationship with God? If yes, how?

_____

_____

_____

TOM'S COMMENT

Absolutely! Their time, energy, and talents are focused on their material possessions and lofty lifestyle instead of their relationship with God. Hence, they have little time to spend with the Lord or serve in ministry.

Angelo's real priorities are his business and money, not his relationship with God, his wife, or his children. Unknowingly, Angelo is enslaved and serves money, not God (Matthew 6:24).

QUESTION #3

Maria enjoys the prestige of owning all these assets and being envied by her friends. Is this indicative of an underlying heart issue? Please provide a reference to Scripture.

_____

_____

_____

TOM'S COMMENT

The fact that Maria relishes being envied is evidence of pride, which God strongly resists. James 4:6 states, "God opposes the proud but shows favor to the humble."

QUESTION #4

How has Angelo and Maria's relationship with God affected how they manage money?

_____

_____

_____

TOM'S COMMENT

Angelo and Maria are not intimately connected to the Lord through a close personal relationship with Him. Consequently, they have developed ungodly attitudes about money and material things and are influenced more by the world and their flesh than by God.

QUESTION #5

What do you believe will be the impact on Angelo and Maria's children? What could their children inadvertently learn about money and material things from their parents?

_____

_____

_____

TOM'S COMMENT

Angelo and Maria's children will likely adopt the same ungodly attitudes toward money and material things as their parents. As a result, they too will probably end up serving money rather than God (Matthew 6:24). As a result, their parents' worldly management of money will more than likely negatively affect their children's relationship with the Lord.

QUESTION #6

What if the future earning abilities of their children are substantially less than Angelo's? What significant challenges could they face as adults because of their upbringing?

_____

_____

_____

TOM'S COMMENT

Their children will probably follow their parents' financial example and adopt the same ungodly desire for money and material things without sufficient income to pay for them. Hence, they will likely spend more than they earn, accumulate debt, and experience financial difficulties.

In addition, they may struggle with a lack of contentment and covetousness, negatively impacting their marriages and their children—Angelo and Maria's future grandchildren.

Angelo's son, in particular, may struggle with self-esteem issues if he does not have his father's high earning capacity and ability to afford the same standard of living for his family. Sadly, as a biblical financial adviser for over four decades, I have seen this too often.

4. Scripture Application #2

Next, discuss the relevance and application of the following Scriptures with respect to Angelo and Maria's situation. Then, write your comments for each verse:

> "Do not wear yourself out to get rich; do not trust your own cleverness. Cast but a glance at riches, and they are gone, for they will surely sprout wings and fly off to the sky like an eagle" (Proverbs 23:4–5).

TOM'S COMMENT

Angelo is burning himself out in pursuit of riches. He is not exercising godly wisdom to get his priorities in proper order—first, his relationship with God, then his wife and children, ministry, and lastly, his business.

> "Since, then, you have been raised with Christ, set your hearts on things above, where Christ is, seated at the right hand of God. Set your minds on things above, not on earthly things" (Colossians 3:1–2).

TOM'S COMMENT

Angelo needs to understand that his business and material possessions are temporary. However, his relationship with God and the service he performs for the Lord have eternal consequences (Matthew 16:27).

Some of these things include loving his wife, training his children in the ways of the Lord (Proverbs 22:6), serving in ministry, and giving to God's work. Therefore, it is vital for Angelo to focus on things of eternal value, not temporal.

When referring to Colossians 3:1–2, what are some examples of "things above"?

_____

_____

_____

TOM'S COMMENT

Among the "things above" would be your relationship with God and doing things that provide eternal benefits, such as living a godly life, loving your spouse, raising your children in the love and admonition of the Lord, giving generously to God's work, and engaging in Christian ministry.

What are some examples of "earthly things"?

_____

_____

_____

TOM'S COMMENT

Some examples of "earthly things" would be Angelo and Maria's money and material possessions, like their thriving business and all of their assets, which are temporary in nature. First Timothy 6:7 says, "We brought nothing into the world, and we can take nothing out of it."

Further, Ecclesiastes 5:15 states, "Everyone comes naked from their mother's womb, and as everyone comes, so they depart. They take nothing from their toil that they can carry in their hands."

TOM'S COMMENT

Angelo and Maria must understand that their earthly pursuit of wealth and riches is temporary and in vain, as everything they acquire has no lasting value in eternity.

"All of you, clothe yourselves with humility toward one another, because, 'God opposes the proud but shows favor to the humble'" (1 Peter 5:5).

TOM'S COMMENT

It is evident from the case study that both Angelo and Maria have a problem with pride and need to learn humility.

5. Case Study #3: A Married Couple Honors God with Their Finances

Steve and Betty have been married for 18 years and have three children. During their first five years of marriage, both worked full-time and lived solely on Steve's income, saving Betty's income for a down payment on a house. To practically accomplish this, they developed and implemented a budget.

As a result of their disciplined savings, they had a substantial down payment when they purchased their first home and, therefore, a relatively small mortgage. They continued to do this for another three years so that when their first child arrived, their mortgage payment was manageable, enabling Betty to stay home to raise their family.

The couple still lives in the same house after 15 years. They are not bothered by the fact that most of their friends and relatives live in nicer homes. Instead, they happily acknowledge that God has met their needs and they frequently thank Him. In addition, they operate with only one used car and have no other debt besides their mortgage, which will be paid off in several years.

Although they are a one-income family, they consistently give the first 10 per cent of their income to God's work. They consistently pray when they have a need, and often God meets that need in an unusual way at either no cost or minimal cost. They praise God for these "little miracles." But, most importantly, Steve and Betty have a solid spiritual life as they spend quality time with the Lord daily and are actively involved in their church.

QUESTION #1

How would you describe Steve and Betty's attitude concerning money and material things? Please provide a Scripture reference for each point, and write your answers before reading Tom's comments and solutions.

_____

_____

_____

TOM'S COMMENT

Steve and Betty's attitude with respect to money and material things can best be described as follows:

- They have a godly attitude because they are content with God's provision (1 Timothy 6:6–8).

- They thank the Lord for what they have (Psalm 107:8–9).

- Their trust and faith are in God alone to meet their needs, evidenced by faithfully giving the first 10 per cent of their increase to God's work despite being a one-income family (Proverbs 3:9–10).

- They are diligent and careful in using the money God has entrusted to them (Proverbs 21:5), as demonstrated by their development and implementation of a budget (Luke 14:28–30).

QUESTION #2

Do you think Steve and Betty's attitude and behaviour concerning managing money and material things have impacted their relationship with God? If so, how?

_____

_____

_____

TOM'S COMMENT

Yes, the couple's attitude toward money and material things and how they managed their money positively impacted their relationship with God.

Since Steve and Betty did not pursue wealth or material possessions but chose to trust in God's provision, they had the time and energy to invest in the things that matter most—their relationship with God, each other, their children, and Christian ministry.

QUESTION #3

As noted, Steve and Betty are not concerned that most of their friends and relatives have nicer homes and newer cars. What heart attitude does this represent?

_____

_____

_____

TOM'S COMMENT

This heart attitude represents contentment, which God values highly. As 1 Timothy 6:6 states, "Godliness with contentment is great gain."

Contentment is an essential godly attitude for a Christian to possess because *contentment is the antidote for worldly attitudes like covetousness, selfishness, and greed.* Unfortunately, these worldly attitudes often lead to unwise decisions, resulting in financial hardship and robbery.

QUESTION #4

What might Steve and Betty's children learn from their parent's example of biblical financial stewardship? How could they be impacted?

_____

_____

_____

TOM'S COMMENT

The impact on Steve and Betty's children will be positive as they will likely adopt a godly perspective on money and material things (Proverbs 22:6). For instance, they will likely be satisfied with God's provision, avoiding serious debt and financial problems.

Further, their biblical approach to managing money and material things will benefit their marriages and children—Steve and Betty's future grandchildren. Proverbs 20:7 states, "The righteous lead blameless lives; blessed are their children after them."

QUESTION #5

In your opinion, has Steve and Betty's close relationship with God affected how they manage money? Please explain.

_____

_____

_____

_____

_____

_____

TOM'S COMMENT

Yes, their close relationship with God led them to develop godly attitudes and behaviours toward money and material things. These include contentment, giving God the first fruits (Proverbs 3:9–10), having minimal debt (Proverbs 22:7), and trusting God for His provision (Psalm 20:7). As a result, they experienced God's peace and joy in their lives, especially their finances (John 14:27).

6. Scripture Application #3

Discuss the relevance and application of the following verses concerning Steve and Betty's situation. Write your comments for each verse.

"I am not saying this because I am in need, for I have learned to be content whatever the circumstances. I know what it is to be in need, and I know what it is to have plenty. I have learned the secret of being content in any and every situation, whether well fed or hungry, whether living in plenty or in want. I can do all this through him who gives me strength" (Philippians 4:11–13).

_____

_____

_____

TOM'S COMMENT

Steve and Betty chose to be content with God's provision and now experience God's peace and joy in their finances. Likewise, their children learn contentment through Steve and Betty's godly example and positive role modeling (Proverbs 22:6).

Consider this important question: What was Paul's "secret" to learning contentment?

_____

_____

_____

TOM'S COMMENT

Paul's secret to learning contentment was to have an intimate relationship with Jesus Christ and focus on things of eternal value, such as evangelism and discipleship (Colossians 3:1–2).

In the same way, you must remain connected to and dependent upon the Lord (John 15:4–8) to learn and maintain an attitude of contentment. Your success will likely be limited if you attempt to do this independently of the Lord.

"Do not worry, saying, 'What shall we eat?' or 'What shall we drink?' or 'What shall we wear?' For the pagans run after all these things, and your heavenly Father knows that you need them. But seek first his kingdom and his righteousness, and all these things will be given to you as well" (Matthew 6:31–33).

_____

_____

_____

TOM'S COMMENT

Steve and Betty put God first by spending quality time with the Lord, each other, and their children. Additionally, they invested in God's work by giving Him the first fruits of all their increase and giving of themselves through regular church ministry. As a result, God faithfully met their needs, even through "little miracles" at times!

7. Case Study #4: A Single Mother Experiences God's Unique Provision

Arlene is a single mother with two children. She works part-time and has a modest income. Although she budgets carefully and spends wisely, her total earnings are significantly less than she needs to support her family.

Over the past few years, God demonstrated His extraordinary power to Arlene by providing in unusual ways. For example, someone from her church gifted her a used car in excellent condition, while a couple rented their basement apartment to her for substantially less than market value.

Another amazing provision is that her children can attend a private Christian school since God specifically moved in the hearts of fellow believers to pay their tuition—some even giving anonymously.

As a result, Arlene learned the truth of Matthew 6:31–33, where Christ promises to meet our needs as we put Him first in managing the money God entrusts to us. Miraculously, all of Arlene's needs and those of her children were met without her having to incur any debt. Praise God, the Lord provided the cash!

During this time, Arlene prayed fervently for God to provide for her and her children. God responded to Arlene similarly to how He fulfilled the needs of the Israelites in the desert (see Exodus 16 and Deuteronomy 28). Therefore, Arlene has many testimonies of God's faithful provision! For example, offers of food, clothing, furnishings, and other necessities have been given to her without her needing to ask. By praying consistently and relying entirely on God, she and her children have had their needs met supernaturally.

On average, Arlene spends quality time with the Lord every morning, which is the best time of her day as she enjoys her fellowship with God. She also has an excellent relationship with her two children, who accepted Jesus Christ as their Saviour and Lord. Further, when meeting Arlene and her children, you can sense their family's love.

Although her earnings are modest, she faithfully gives 10 per cent of her income to the Lord's work. Most people would find this impossible, but Arlene sees it as a way to honor God and demonstrate her faith and trust in Him. Despite a tight budget and basic lifestyle, Arlene and her children are satisfied with God's provision and praise the Lord for their many blessings.

QUESTION #1

How would you describe Arlene's attitude concerning money and material things? Please provide a similar example from the Bible.

_____

_____

_____

TOM'S COMMENT

Arlene is a godly woman, demonstrated by her unwavering trust in the Lord to meet her family's needs. Additionally, she and her children are content with God's provision. Arlene is like the widow in Luke 21 who gave all she had to God, and the widow in 2 Kings 4, whom God miraculously provided oil through Elisha so she could pay her debts.

QUESTION #2

Do you think Arlene's attitude and behaviour regarding money and material things impact her relationship with God? If so, how?

_____

_____

_____

TOM'S COMMENT

Yes, absolutely. As Arlene prays and relies solely on God to provide for her family, she is drawn closer to the Lord (John 15:4–8). Further, giving 10 per cent of her increase out of a meager income reflects her trust and faith in God. *The more she trusts God, the closer her relationship with God becomes.*

QUESTION #3

Similarly, do you believe Arlene's intimate relationship with God affects the stewardship of her finances? Please explain.

_____

_____

_____

TOM'S COMMENT

Most definitely. It is doubtful a single mother would give 10 per cent of her income to God's work unless she had a close relationship with the Lord. Her tithing is sacrificial giving, which is rare in our day.

In addition, because of her intimacy with God, she has learned to be content with a modest lifestyle (Philippians 4:11–13). As a result, Arlene experiences God's peace and joy in her finances, notwithstanding her challenging situation (Romans 8:6).

Because of Arlene's close relationship with the Lord and her consistent prayer life, God has provided generously. For example, her children attend a Christian school, and she rents an apartment for much less than she would otherwise have to pay.

QUESTION #4

From Arlene's example of financial management and her daily Christian walk, what valuable lessons will her children likely learn?

_____

_____

_____

TOM'S COMMENT

Arlene's children will likely learn many biblical principles and godly attitudes concerning finances and righteous living. These include contentment (Luke 3:14), the power of prayer, depending solely on God for provision (Matthew 6:31–33), generosity through giving, and experiencing God's peace and joy in finances regardless of income (John 14:27).

QUESTION #5

Assuming Arlene's children end up with modest incomes in adulthood, how do you think they would manage?

_____

_____

_____

_____

_____

_____

TOM'S COMMENT

A modest income would likely be fine for Arlene's children, thanks to their upbringing and their mother's godly example. They would probably trust God for His provision, be content with a basic lifestyle, and regularly give to the Lord's work.

8. Scripture Application #4

Discuss the relevance and application of the following verses concerning Arlene's situation. Write your comments for each verse.

"Some trust in chariots and some in horses, but we trust in the name of the Lord our God" (Psalm 20:7).

_____

_____

_____

TOM'S COMMENT

Arlene trusted in God alone to provide for her needs. She did not trust in her income-earning capacity or rely on credit to pay her bills. Instead, she fully trusted God to provide all she needed without having to incur debt, and praise God, the Lord did!

"Those who trust in the Lord are like Mount Zion, which cannot be shaken but endures forever. As the mountains surround Jerusalem, so the Lord surrounds his people both now and forevermore" (Psalm 125:1–2).

_____

_____

_____

TOM'S COMMENT

Arlene was not "shaken" or worried about her finances; instead, she experienced God's peace and joy as she trusted in Him. God cared for Arlene and her family, protected them, and provided for their every need.

"Honor the LORD with your wealth, with the firstfruits of all your crops; then your barns will be filled to overflowing, and your vats will brim over with new wine" (Proverbs 3:9–10).

_____

_____

_____

TOM'S COMMENT

Arlene honored God with her income by giving the first 10 per cent out of her modest income to God's kingdom work. As a result, God performed many miracles in providing for her family's needs.

In this sense, Arlene's "barns were filled to overflowing" as she was blessed and able to send her children to a private Christian school, which would have been impossible without God's supernatural provision.

"Godliness with contentment is great gain. For we brought nothing into the world, and we can take nothing out of it. But if we have food and clothing, we will be content with that" (1 Timothy 6:6–8).

_____

_____

_____

TOM'S COMMENT

Arlene and her children are content with having their basic needs met. God's word says that godliness with contentment is great gain because it leads to things of greater value than money and material things. In Arlene's case, these include a close personal relationship with the Lord and an excellent relationship with her two children, who follow God's ways and store up their own treasures in heaven (Matthew 6:19–21).

> "Give thanks to the LORD, for he is good; his love endures forever" (Psalm 118:1).

_____

_____

_____

TOM'S COMMENT

Although Arlene and her children live a very modest lifestyle, what they have is more precious—a genuine personal relationship with the Lord and each other. They regularly thank God for His faithfulness in caring for them and experience His peace and joy in every aspect of their lives.

> "May the God of hope fill you with all joy and peace as you trust in him, so that you may overflow with hope by the power of the Holy Spirit" (Romans 15:13).

_____

_____

_____

TOM'S COMMENT

The *God of hope* has filled Arlene and her children with His joy and peace as they demonstrate their trust in Him. However, most people would not rejoice in similar circumstances because they would desire more than they had. Therefore, it is essential to maintain a close personal relationship with Jesus Christ and rely on the Holy Spirit to enable you to be content.

9. Ten Essential Money Management Steps to Strengthen Your Relationship with God

What practical steps can a believer take to ensure their relationship with the Lord is strengthened rather than hindered by their management of money and material possessions? Please provide a reference to Scripture for each point as you are able.

_____

_____

_____

The following is a list of the ten most essential steps a Christian should take to ensure their relationship with God is strengthened, rather than hindered, by their management of money and material things:

- Pray and seek God's wisdom (James 1:5) and direction (Psalm 32:8) before making significant financial decisions.

- Engage in the regular study of God's word on finances, such as reading appropriate books and participating in small-group classes, like my in-depth biblical financial study, "Financial Management God's Way." Our small groups are primarily online, so you can participate no matter where you live.

67

- If you are in business, I recommend you watch my eight TV programs, "God's Financial Wisdom for Business." For more details, visit www.coplandfinancialministries.org.

- Meditate on Scriptures that address specific areas of struggle. Chapter IV (Developing Godly Attitudes Toward Money) provides appropriate verses that deal with specific problems. For example, if you struggle with covetousness, meditate on Exodus 20:17, which specifically warns against covetousness. For issues related to contentment, meditate on Luke 3:14; Philippians 4:11–13; and 1 Timothy 6:6–8.

- Spend quality time with God in prayer every day, listening for His gentle whisper (1 Kings 19:11–13), and hearing God's voice (John 10:27).

- Seek godly counsel on significant financial decisions (Proverbs 12:15, Psalm 1:1–3).

- Develop and implement a budget (Luke 14:28–30).

- Recognize that God owns everything (1 Chronicles 29:11–12).

- Thank God regularly for His provision (Psalm 107:8–9).

- Give generously to God's work with a cheerful heart (2 Corinthians 9:6–7).

- Develop a godly attitude toward money and material things (chapter IV).

Based on my experience as a Christian financial adviser for over four decades, I am confident your relationship with God will be strengthened if you faithfully follow these ten steps.

Furthermore, as you learn and apply these biblically-based financial principles, you will positively impact your relationship with your spouse, your children, and indirectly your grandchildren and others.

10. Developing a Budget

I encourage you to begin recording your expenditures if you are not already doing so. A free download of the Copland Budgeting System is on our website, www.coplandfinancialministries.org. Additionally, a 30-minute video explains how to use the budgeting tool.

After you have recorded your expenses on form #6 (I suggest you do this for six months), total each category and divide by 6 to give you the average monthly cost for a particular category. Then prepare form #5, which will give you an idea of your typical monthly budget—what you have spent versus your income. You can then determine if you typically have a positive or negative monthly cash flow.

There is no substitute for having a "pulse" on what is happening with your finances. Unfortunately, most people unintentionally spend more than they earn and accumulate debt, which is not God's desire for His people.

According to biblical financial principles, God wants us to develop a cash flow plan (a budget) to ensure we spend less than we earn. This way, we will have a monthly surplus to pay down debt and save for future needs.

As Proverbs 21:5 points out, "The plans of the diligent lead to profit as surely as haste leads to poverty." Likewise, Proverbs

21:20 states, "The wise man saves for the future, but the foolish man spends whatever he gets" (TLB).

11. Summary: Management of Money Impacts Your Relationship with God

From the Scriptures provided and real-life case studies, it is clear that how you manage money directly impacts your relationship with God. The reverse is also true: your relationship with God affects how you manage money. There is no refuting that the two are strongly interconnected.

In the next chapter, I will discuss how money management impacts your relationship with your spouse and others.

II.

MANAGEMENT OF MONEY IMPACTS YOUR RELATIONSHIP WITH YOUR SPOUSE, CHILDREN, AND OTHERS

A. KEY QUESTIONS AND TOM'S COMMENTS

QUESTION #1

Here's something to consider. Does the way you manage money impact your relationship with your spouse, *or* is your relationship independent of how you manage money? If you are single, this principle is still important to understand should God bring you a spouse.

Before you read Tom's comments, please write your thoughts and provide some Scriptural references as able.

_____

_____

_____

TOM'S COMMENT

According to Genesis 2:24, a husband and wife are "one flesh." Therefore, whatever affects one spouse will affect the other.

I receive a call from a husband or wife almost weekly stating that they are in serious financial trouble. Typically, one or both spouses have violated God's financial principles—most commonly by spending too much and accumulating debt, often resulting in arguments between the couple. Inevitably, as their debt increases, the stress between them increases, eventually destroying the relationship.

QUESTION #2

Interestingly, even though I am an accountant and financial adviser, *not* a marriage counselor, couples often share their struggles and marriage problems without me even asking. Why do you think this is?

Please reflect on this and write your thoughts before reading my comments.

TOM'S COMMENT

Many couples talk to me about their marriage problems when they seek financial counseling because finances and marital relationships are closely interconnected! Unfortunately, most couples only realize this once they start arguing regularly about money and related issues.

1. Do Not Ignore Financial Problems!

About a third of those we minister to at Copland Financial Ministries are separated or divorced. Almost always, finances are the main issue they and their ex-spouse argued about. In most cases, there was enough income, but either one or both managed money *the world's way rather than God's way, causing financial tension and hardship.*

My advice to couples is to *never ignore financial problems because they can destroy your marriage in the long run!* Proverbs 22:3 states, "The prudent see danger and take refuge, but the simple keep going and pay the penalty."

Further, most surveys indicate that finances were the most common subject of disagreement for separated or divorced couples. Is there a solution to this problem? If so, what is the solution?

_____

_____

_____

TOM'S COMMENT

Absolutely, there is a solution for a husband and wife to avoid stress and arguments over finances! Conceptually, the answer is simple. Both need to learn and apply God's way of managing money. Specifically, a husband and wife need to do the following:

- Regularly study God's word on finances (2 Timothy 3:16–17).

- Meditate on key Scriptures (Joshua 1:8).

- Allow God, through His Spirit and His Word (Hebrews 4:12) to change how they think about money and material things (Romans 12:2).

Following these biblical financial principles will result in long-term changes in how couples manage money. Sadly, in my experience, most Christians do not manage money God's way because they have limited knowledge of what God's word says about finances.

Interestingly, of the 2,350 references to money and material things in the Bible, only about 3 per cent deal with giving, while 97 per cent deal with other financial topics that most Christians have never learned. These include the following:

- The dangers of debt (Proverbs 22:7).

- God's warning to plan ahead, which includes following a budget (Luke 14:28–30).

- The difference between a godly attitude and mindset and a worldly attitude and mindset concerning money (see chapter IV of this book for details).

- The importance of saving for future needs (Proverbs 21:20).

- How money management impacts eternity (Matthew 16:27 and Matthew 6:19–21; see Chapter V of this book).

- How to experience God's peace in your finances (Philippians 4:4–7).

- The distinction between "financial deceptions" of the world versus "financial truths" in God's word (see chapter V of this book and chapter V of my book *Debt Reduction: Biblical Principles to Deal with Inflation, High Interest Rates, and Eliminating Debt*).

Remember that Jesus told His disciples in John 8:31–32, "If you hold to my teaching, you are really my disciples. Then you will know the truth, and the truth will set you free." Knowing and applying God's truth with respect to finances will set you free from the "financial deceptions" of this world and from the bondage of financial problems.

2. Financial Temptations

Almost everyone has at least one area where they spend too much money, which I call a "financial temptation."

QUESTION #3

What are some common financial temptations or pitfalls for women?

_____

_____

_____

TOM'S COMMENT

In my experience, women generally struggle with financial temptation or fall short when it comes to their finances in these areas:

1. To satisfy their wants and desires, women often spend too much money on personal grooming such as makeup, hair styling, clothing, shoes, jewelry, home décor, and things for their children. To expand on this, many women define themselves by their physical appearance. Therefore, they may spend a great deal on outward adornments to enhance that identity. However, God has a different perspective and standard of beauty, as revealed in 1 Peter 3:3–4:

   "Your beauty should not come from outward adornment, such as elaborate hairstyles and the wearing of gold jewelry or fine clothes. Rather, it should be that of your inner self, the unfading

75

beauty of a gentle and quiet spirit, which is of great worth in God's sight."

In other words, God prioritizes a woman's godly character over her physical appearance.

2. In some cases, excessive spending can be an attempt to satisfy an emotional need or void. For instance, a woman may struggle with marital problems or unresolved trauma from childhood.

   Resolving these underlying issues as soon as possible is best rather than allowing continued overspending. Remember that God has promised to meet our needs, not necessarily our wants and desires (Matthew 6:31–33).

3. Another financial temptation for some women is the desire to purchase a larger and more expensive home than is necessary (1 Timothy 6:6–8).

   Sometimes a woman's identity comes from her home, which may be reflected through excessive interior decorating. However, a woman's core identity should come from her personal relationship with God, not her home. In such cases, there may be a need to learn contentment (Philippians 4:11–13).

4. Investing is an area where many women need more knowledge, especially concerning the principles of biblical investing. At a minimum, women need to learn the basics of what the Bible says about investing.

   If this applies to you, please consider viewing the three 28-minute teachings, "Investing God's Way," on our ministry website, www.coplandfinancialministries.org.

5. It can be risky for a husband to assume full responsibility for the household finances when his wife has limited knowledge of them. For example, the wife could be left in a precarious position if her husband became incapacitated or the relationship ended for any reason.

At the very least, a woman should have a general knowledge of their monthly household income and expenses, key documents such as their wills, power of attorney, mortgage, bank accounts, and investment portfolios. Proverbs 24:3–4 says, "By wisdom a house is built, and through understanding it is established; through knowledge its rooms are filled with rare and beautiful treasures."

QUESTION #4

What are some common financial temptations or pitfalls for men?

_____

_____

_____

TOM'S COMMENT

In my experience, the most common areas where men struggle with financial temptation or fall short in their finances are:

- Spending too much money on their automobile or truck. For some men, their vehicle is a part of their identity. As Christians, our identity should come from who we are in Christ Jesus (Genesis 1:27), not from the things we own.

- Some men are "tool guys" and fall into the temptation to want the best and latest tools, spending more than necessary. They need to be aware of this temptation and avoid it (1 Corinthians 10:13).

- Some "boys like their toys," such as boats, four-wheelers, motorcycles, or electronics. These are generally expensive items that can rack up debt fast.

- Some men spend too much on sporting items or events, like golf clubs, membership dues, and athletic clubs.

- Some men are risk-takers and too comfortable with borrowing money to invest. It is important to remember that God discourages debt (Proverbs 22:7). The biblical way to save for medium and long-term needs is to save a little at a time (Proverbs 13:11) over a long period (Proverbs 21:5).

  Recall that in Deuteronomy 28, God consistently met the needs of His people with *no debt*! For example, a husband should never use the family home to secure an investment. If the investment fails, it could result in serious financial problems, a destroyed marriage, and a negative impact on the children.

- Some men are not open to financial counsel due to embarrassment and pride (1 Peter 5:5) or because they believe they can handle their financial problems on their own. Unfortunately, most men do not understand that accumulating debt can negatively affect their relationships with their wives on a physical, emotional, and spiritual level (Ephesians 5:28).

- Men often find their core identity in their work. But, as with women, their identity should be rooted primarily in their relationship with God.

Finding a healthy balance between one's spiritual, family, and work life can be challenging for many men. For example, it is not uncommon for a husband to prioritize providing for his family's financial and material needs while neglecting his wife's and children's spiritual and emotional needs.

However, Ephesians 5:25–28 commands husbands to love their wives in a sacrificial way, such as developing a close emotional and spiritual relationship with her. In other words, cultivating a meaningful relationship with her that goes beyond a physical and material connection.

To summarize, our core identity as men and women of God must come from our relationship with Jesus Christ. We must never forget that we are first and foremost God's child, created in His divine image (Genesis 1:27), and unconditionally loved by the Lord.

3. Identifying Your Areas of Financial Temptation

The above is just a general list. The most important thing that individuals need to ask themselves is *"what are my areas of financial temptation?"*

In other words, in what areas do you tend to mismanage money and spend more than you should? In what areas do you need to learn more about God's way of managing money?

In Psalm 139:23–24, David prayed, "Search me, O God, and know my heart; test me and know my anxious thoughts. See if there is any offensive way in me, and lead me in the way everlasting."

I encourage you to pray the same way and ask God by His Holy Spirit to reveal your areas of "financial temptations," and then write them here.

_____

_____

_____

TOM'S COMMENT

I highly recommend you meditate upon 1 Corinthians 10:13, where Paul said:

> "No temptation has overtaken you except what is common to mankind. And God is faithful; he will not let you be tempted beyond what you can bear. But when you are tempted, he will also provide a way out so that you can endure it."

To put it another way, *steer clear of your areas of financial temptation!* For example, if you're a car enthusiast, don't visit your local dealership to check out the latest models! Likewise, if you're a woman who enjoys spending money at the mall, avoid going there to browse. If you must go, have a list and focus on getting only what you need; then leave. Refrain from window shopping!

Here is a word of caution for everyone about the temptation of online shopping. This convenience makes it too easy to spend beyond your means with just a few clicks of the mouse. Unchecked, this habit can lead you to spend money you don't have on things you don't need, contributing to financial difficulties and stress in your marriage.

Please understand I have given generalizations in my comments. I realize some men have problems at the shopping mall, and some women like to kick tires. The bottom line is this: whatever your particular area of financial temptation, do what you must to avoid it!

Another important recommendation is to be aware that our flesh, the world, and Satan continually try to "lead us into temptation" and entice us to buy things we don't need. Therefore, as soon as the first tempting thought enters your mind, *take that thought captive to the obedience of Christ!* (2 Corinthians 10:5). In other words, immediately reject the thought and prayerfully focus on God, asking Him for the ability to be content without that item (Philippians 4:11–13).

4. Communicating About Finances

It is vital for husbands and wives to communicate with each other about their finances in an honest and transparent way. This is especially true before making any significant financial purchase or commitment. For instance, even if you bought something you needed but neglected to develop a budget to ensure you could afford it, and you did not obtain your spouse's approval, your decision to go ahead and purchase that item could lead to marital tension and problems.

I cannot emphasize enough that buying things you don't need and accumulating debt can destroy your emotional, physical, and spiritual relationship with your spouse. Unfortunately, however, most poor money managers have no idea that their mismanagement of money can ruin their marriage relationship until it's too late and the relationship has disintegrated to the point of separation and divorce.

One of the objectives of Copland Financial Ministries is to help couples avoid the financial fallout that typically occurs when one or both partners knowingly or unknowingly violate God's financial principles.

B. CASE STUDY, QUESTIONS, TOM'S COMMENTS

1. Complex Case Study: A Saver Married to a Spender

Please note that in this case study, I have intentionally not identified the "Spender" or "Saver" with any particular gender.

While counseling clients on financial matters for many years, I've seen as many men as women who were spenders and as many women as men who were savers. Sadly, the following scenario represents a situation I see all too often among couples.

Spender and Saver are married. Saver manages money God's way, including saving for future needs (see Proverbs 21:20). Unfortunately, Spender manages money according to worldly standards.

Although the couple has sufficient income to live a comfortable middle-class lifestyle, Spender spends money faster than Saver can save money! As a result, over just a few years, Spender accumulates significant debt along with a bad credit rating.

When the couple renews their mortgage, the bank runs their usual credit check, revealing Spender's out-of-control credit card debt, which was unknown to Saver. Consequently, the couple incurs a much higher interest rate at the time of their mortgage renewal.

Notwithstanding, Spender ignores any financial advice and continues to purchase material things they do not need, mainly using credit. In short, Spender is *un*willing to change their financial management habits or to learn how to manage money God's way.

QUESTION #1

How would you feel if your spouse accumulated significant debt without your knowledge?

_____

_____

_____

TOM'S COMMENT

Most people would feel cheated and betrayed, causing significant strain in their relationship. In addition, accumulating debt without your spouse's knowledge can destroy trust, which is essential for a healthy marriage. As previously stated, most spenders are unaware that their irresponsible use of money will inevitably damage their relationship and possibly lead to separation or divorce.

As noted in Proverbs 12:13, "The wicked are trapped by their own words, but the godly escape such trouble" (NLT). Further, Titus 2:7 says, "In everything set them an example by doing what is good. In your teaching show integrity."

QUESTION #2

What should Saver do? Suggest some interventions, proceeding from one step to the next if Spender refuses to cut back on their unnecessary spending and debt accumulation.

Next, provide a Scripture reference for each point, and note Tom's 15-step process that could take two to three years to complete if Spender does not respond to the interventions, squandering more money.

_____

_____

_____

_____

_____

_____

_____

_____

_____

_____

_____

_____

TOM'S COMMENT

The first step any Christian should take when faced with a difficult decision, including a financial one or needing to approach a spouse about a sensitive matter, is to pray and ask God for His wisdom (James 1:5), His specific direction (Psalm 32:8), and perfect timing in each step.

1. Pray and ask God to change the spender's heart with respect to managing money. Proverbs 21:1 says, "In

the LORD's hand the king's heart is a stream of water that he channels toward all who please him."

2. Hebrews 4:12 tells us, "The word of God is alive and active. Sharper than any double-edged sword." Therefore, Saver and a godly friend should graciously present God's word to Spender regarding finances, as the Lord directs.

3. As the Holy Spirit opens the door, Saver should explain to Spender that their excessive spending (Ecclesiastes 5:11) has caused serious financial problems and negatively affected their relationship. Show evidence of increasing debt levels, such as credit card statements, to demonstrate that they have been spending more than they earn, thus accumulating debt.

4. Provide Spender with appropriate resources that teach God's word on finances (like a CD, DVD, and books) since God directs and guides us through His word (Psalm 119:105). Please give them a copy of this book, for example.

5. Encourage Spender to attend a small group financial Bible study (2 Timothy 3:16–17), such as my in-depth study "Financial Management God's Way." In addition, our ministry offers many workshops on Zoom so you can participate no matter where you live. To register for a seminar, visit www.coplandfinancialministries.org.

6. Consult a godly financial adviser for Spender and Saver (Psalms 1:1–3).

7. Prayerfully discern the presence of an underlying spiritual battle (Ephesians 6:10–18) and address it

appropriately (2 Corinthians 10:4–5). Spiritual warfare is generally conducted through prayer and the revelation of God's truth. Therefore, Spender must learn the truth of God's word concerning finances to counter Satan's primary weapon of deception (John 8:31–32).

8. Ask trusted friends and members of your church to confidentially pray for Spender, Saver, and their children (1 Thessalonians 5:25).

9. Saver should continue to manage money God's way, setting a godly example for Spender and their children (Proverbs 22:6).

10. Have a relative or friend who understands God's word on finances and whom Spender respects provide godly counsel to Spender. Proverbs 27:6 says, "Wounds from a friend can be trusted, but an enemy multiplies kisses."

11. If Spender continues to spend irresponsibly, you can limit their debt accumulation by restricting access to joint credit cards or lines of credit (Romans 13:8). In other words, exercise some *tough love* if Spender ignores all the advice and continues to waste money.

12. If necessary, exercise more tough love by assuming control of the household finances (1 Timothy 5:8). For example, set up a separate bank account in Saver's name to ensure sufficient funds to cover necessities such as food, utilities, transportation, life insurance premiums, and mortgage payments.

13. During your prayer time, if the Lord reveals that your marriage is under spiritual attack, obtain godly counsel from a mature Christian familiar with strategic warfare.

Although the enemy plots to destroy marriages, remember, "The one who is in you is greater than the one who is in the world" (1 John 4:4). Praise God! The Holy Spirit who lives in you is more powerful than Satan and his demons. Further, according to Luke 10:19, God gives us the authority to "trample on snakes and scorpions and to overcome all the power of the enemy; nothing will harm you."

14. Saver should wait patiently on the Lord (Psalm 37:7), but if Spender continues to violate biblical principles of financial management and accumulates more debt (especially if the needs of the family are threatened), consider the following call to action as outlined in Matthew 18:15–17:

> "If your brother or sister sins, go and point out their fault, just between the two of you. If they listen to you, you have won them over. But if they will not listen, take one or two others along, so that 'every matter may be established by the testimony of two or three witnesses.' If they still refuse to listen, tell it to the church; and if they refuse to listen even to the church, treat them as you would a pagan or a tax collector."

I highly recommend that the "one or two others" be godly individuals who understand God's word on finances and the seriousness of debt.

15. It is prudent for Saver to warn Spender before approaching the church leaders. If Spender refuses to change, it may be necessary to have their church elders pray, counsel, and admonish them. The goal is

not to offend Spender but to get them to change their destructive financial habits.

If nothing is done, it is usually only a matter of time before the family suffers severe consequences, such as the repossession of their vehicle, loss of utilities, or a home foreclosure.

In other words, the family's basic needs are no longer being met due to Spender's ungodly money habits. This is contrary to God's word in 1 Timothy 5:8, which states, "Anyone who does not provide for their relatives, and especially for their own household, has denied the faith and is worse than an unbeliever."

Even if your spouse is not a Christian, it is still sensible to follow Matthew 18 conceptually by getting someone your spouse respects and is an effective money manager to talk to Spender about their excessive spending. Proverbs 22:3 says, "The prudent see danger and take refuge, but the simple keep going and pay the penalty."

If you identify with this case study, it is imperative that you address the problem rather than waiting until you lose your home or are forced into personal bankruptcy. In most cases, this leads to separation and divorce. Take every measure available to you to avoid this.

2. Biblical Financial Advice for Engaged Couples

Most couples neglect to discuss finances in depth before marrying. Instead, they assume that their love for each other will overcome any future problems they may encounter, including financial difficulties.

Additionally, they often assume their management of money will have minimal impact on their relationship. However, *this is not true!* As previously stated, how you manage money will tremendously impact your future marriage.

With that in mind, if you're engaged to be married or thinking of marrying one day, I encourage you to consider the following biblical financial advice:

- Before marrying, I recommend *full disclosure* of all debts by both parties. This is vital because "debt surprises" can cause conflict and serious problems after the wedding. One spouse may feel deceived or cheated by the other, who brought significant debt into the new marriage. As a practical matter, your debt becomes your spouse's debt, and their debt becomes yours.

- Couples must have an open and honest conversation about lifestyle expectations, followed by preparing a budget to determine if those expectations are affordable. If not, they will need to learn to be content and develop a realistic budget and lifestyle based on what they can afford (Philippians 4:11–13).

- As a Christian couple, consider taking a course on biblically-based financial management—like my in-depth series, "Financial Management God's Way." When you learn God's word on finances and agree to manage money His way, your marriage will be strengthened, and you will have a solid foundation to build your life together. Besides saving you from potential grief, this will provide a powerful testimony for others and honor the Lord greatly.

Our ministry offers some excellent resources for those who are engaged to be married or considering marriage. For instance, I encourage you to watch our 18-minute video "Biblical Financial Advice for Engaged Couples". This can be seen on our ministry website, www.coplandfinancialministries.org.

Additionally, our website offers eight 28-minute programs on "God's Financial Wisdom for Young People," which have helped thousands of others.

The same website also offers a free download of the Excel-based Copland Budgeting System and a 30-minute video explaining how to use the budgeting tool.

3. Management of Money Impacts Relationships with Your Children

QUESTION #1

Does the way parents manage money impact how their children are likely to manage money as adults?

_____

_____

_____

TOM'S COMMENT

Without a doubt, the way parents manage money can have a significant and lasting impact on how their children will manage money. Proverbs 22:6 states, "Train up a child in the way he should go; even when he is old he will not depart from it" (ESV).

Whether intended or not, parents set a financial example for their children, which can be positive or negative. Put another way, their role modeling could reflect a biblical or worldly perspective on financial stewardship.

For example, I have seen many cases of parents managing their money the world's way—spending more than they earn, accumulating debt, causing tension between the mother and father, and receiving calls from creditors. Unfortunately, this is a common occurrence in their homes.

Thus, many young adults unwittingly follow their parents' ungodly example of managing money. Inadvertently, they are at greater risk of experiencing similar financial and marital problems in adulthood as their parents.

However, I've seen many cases where parents have managed money according to biblical principles, where they:

- Develop and follow a budget (Proverbs 21:5).

- Are content to live within their means (Luke 3:14).

- Save for future needs (Proverbs 21:20).

- Put God first in managing money (Matthew 6:31–33).

- Pray and trust God to meet their needs (Proverbs 3:5–6; Philippians 4:19).

For parents who teach their children the biblical principles of financial management, it will impact not only their children but, very likely, their future grandchildren, great-grandchildren, and so on.

4. Suggestions for Teaching Children God's Way of Managing Money

In the early years of a child's life, and when they receive an allowance or gifts from family members, parents could provide them with three jars as follows:

- Jar #1 for giving—the guideline is 10 per cent of their increase.

- Jar #2 for saving—I suggest at least a 40 per cent contribution.

- Jar # 3 for spending—I recommend a 50 per cent contribution.

As adults, children who are taught to give (Proverbs 3:9–10), to save (Proverbs 13:11), and to limit their spending, will likely be effective money managers and experience God's peace (John 14:27) in their finances.

However, what do most children do when they get money? *They usually spend it all!* Consequently, they will likely perpetuate the same habits in adulthood if they don't learn the value of giving and saving while young.

Further, once they have a job and income, the banks and credit card companies will be more than happy to lend them money, enabling them to spend even more and accumulate debt.

Therefore, parents are responsible for teaching their children about the dangers of debt (Proverbs 22:7) and providing them with clear biblical guidelines. For example, once children are a little older, they must understand it is not a sin to borrow for major purchases like a car or a house, if necessary. However, they need to be aware of the risk of snowballing debt, which can become overwhelming and result in many hardships.

Another critical point is that before taking on any debt, they need to learn how to develop and maintain a budget to ensure they have sufficient income to repay their loans.

Finally, parents are advised to teach their children the difference between a want or desire and a need, and to explain that *God will meet their needs if they put Him first, but not necessarily their wants or desires.* In Matthew 6:25–34, Jesus said:

"Therefore I tell you, do not worry about your life, what you will eat or drink; or about your body, what you will wear. Is not life more than food, and the body more than clothes? Look at the birds of the air; they do not sow or reap or store away in barns, and yet your heavenly Father feeds them. Are you not much more valuable than they? Can any one of you by worrying add a single hour to your life?

"And why do you worry about clothes? See how the flowers of the field grow. They do not labor or spin. Yet I tell you that not even Solomon in all his splendor was dressed like one of these. If that is how God clothes the grass of the field, which is here today and tomorrow is thrown into the fire, will he not much more clothe you— you of little faith? So do not worry, saying, 'What shall we eat?' or 'What shall we drink?' or 'What shall we wear?' For the pagans run after all these things, and your heavenly Father knows that you need them. But seek first his kingdom and his righteousness, and all these things will be given to you as well. Therefore do not worry about tomorrow, for tomorrow will worry about itself. Each day has enough trouble of its own."

To parents reading this book, I strongly encourage you to meditate on the words of Jesus in Matthew 6:25–34. It is an absolute promise from the God of the universe that if we put Him first, *He will meet our needs!* So we need not fret or worry but simply trust Him, take Him at His word, and stand in faith.

Jeremiah 17:7 reminds us, "Blessed is the one who trusts in the LORD, whose confidence is in him." Further, Psalm 37:3 says, "Trust in the LORD and do good; dwell in the land and enjoy safe pasture."

5. Impact of Money Management on Family Members, Friends, and Others

QUESTION #1

Do you think that how friends and family members manage money could impact you? If you agree, please provide some reasons why.

_____

_____

_____

TOM'S COMMENT

The answer is yes, and here are my thoughts: When people knowingly or unknowingly violate biblical financial principles, they usually accumulate debt. As a result, it is common for them to turn to family members or friends for help, usually in the form of a loan. However, these loans are often not repaid because the borrower has been irresponsible and managed money the world's way. Inevitably, unrepaid loans create tension between family members and friends, negatively affecting their relationships.

The concern about providing a loan to a bad money manager is that it typically deals with the symptom and not the underlying problem—that the individual or couple generally mismanage their money, spend beyond what they make, and accumulate debt. Unfortunately, their poor financial habits are likely to continue unless they learn to apply God's principles of managing money.

Therefore, in some cases, when you lend money to another in debt, you may be *enabling them* to continue with their poor financial habits. In Luke 16:10, Jesus said, "The *one* faithful in very little is also faithful in much, and the *one* unrighteous in very little is also unrighteous in much" (Berean Literal Bible).

Therefore, when a friend or family member comes to you requesting a loan, I encourage you to pray and ask God for discernment on whether or not to loan them money. Although denying the loan may seem unkind, it may be in their best inter-est and for their ultimate good. More often than not, people need to learn how to manage their finances more effectively.

Aside from lending money, one constructive way to help is to direct them to resources that will teach them sound, biblical-ly-based financial principles. For example, you could connect them to our website at www.coplandfinancialministries.org, which offers a variety of resources that teach biblical principles of financial management.

Alternatively, if you feel confident in your knowledge, you could share what you have learned through your personal jour-ney of learning how to manage money God's way.

QUESTION #2

Aside from harming personal relationships, what other negative repercussions are associated with accumulating debt? Please think about this, then write your thoughts and any real-life examples you have encountered.

_____

_____

_____

TOM'S COMMENT

There can be many adverse outcomes when an individual or couple accumulates debt, especially when their debt exceeds what they can afford. When this occurs, their credit rating will inevitably suffer, which can result in the following consequences:

- A lender, typically a bank, can refuse to approve a mortgage at the time of renewal, resulting in the loss of one's home or dependency on costly private financing.

- A landlord can reject a rental application, as most landlords run a credit check.

- Lost job opportunities can occur, especially for management positions, since most employers check a prospective employee's credit history. For example, I recall a gentleman who went through several interviews for a senior manager position at a high-profile organization. He had the right experience, the right skills, and the proper education. After his references were checked, a formal letter was drafted offering him a substantial salary with excellent benefits, pending a credit check. But unfortunately, he and his wife were terrible at managing their money, as revealed by the credit report. Sadly, he lost out on a fabulous employment opportunity because of poor money management practices.

• When a follower of Christ doesn't pay their debts on time or defaults on payment, they will have a flawed testimony. This is a serious matter because, according to Psalm 37:21, "The wicked borrow and do not repay, but the righteous give generously." In other words, the Bible is clear that refusing to repay debt reveals a wicked heart, not the generous and giving heart the Lord wants His people to have. Further, in Matthew 5:14–16, Jesus said:

> "You are the light of the world. A town built on a hill cannot be hidden. Neither do people light a lamp and put it under a bowl. Instead they put it on its stand, and it gives light to everyone in the house. In the same way, *let your light shine before others, that they may see your good deeds and glorify your Father in heaven*" (emphasis added).

What kind of a light in a world of darkness is a Christian who does not pay their debts on time, especially if they do not repay at all? It provides a bad witness to others and dishonors the Lord as it violates His moral character and biblical principles of financial management.

6. In Summary: Management of Money Impacts Your Relationship with Your Spouse, Children, and Others

The purpose of this chapter is to help you better understand and appreciate that how you handle money can negatively or positively impact your relationship with your spouse and others.

For example, let's say both husband and wife learn and apply biblical financial principles and wait patiently for the Lord to reveal what He wants them to do, especially b*efore making any major financial decisions. In that case,* God will direct them (Psalm 32:8), and bless them (Matthew 25:14–30), so that their finances will be an area of peace, unity, and agreement in their marriage, not an area of stress, as it is in many marriages.

Further, parents need to manage money according to biblical principles and provide a solid biblical example concerning money management to their children. This will provide their children with a firm foundation on which to start their financial lives, indirectly affecting future generations. Proverbs 22:6 says, "Start children off on the way they should go, and even when they are old they will not turn from it."

In addition, how an individual or couple manages money can impact relationships with family members and friends, particularly if they get into debt and borrow from various people—especially if they do not repay their personal loans.

Finally, if people mismanage money, this will be reflected in their credit rating. Some consequences of a poor credit rating are getting turned down for loans (like a premortgage approval), being ineligible to rent a place, and missing out on excellent employment opportunities. But most significantly, the chronic misuse of your finances could result in a flawed testimony for the Lord and a compromised relationship with Him.

In conclusion, make it your priority to manage money biblically to preserve your relationship with your spouse, children, friends, potential employers, and creditors. In this way, you will maintain your testimony for the Lord, which is honoring to God.

Moreover, managing money according to God's financial principles, as outlined in His word, the Bible, is a wise decision!

III.

GOD'S PROMISES AND OUR STEWARDSHIP RESPONSIBILITIES

A. OBJECTIVE OF THIS CHAPTER

To better understand God's promises and our responsibilities concerning the management of money and material things.

B. KEY BIBLICAL PRINCIPLE AND SCRIPTURE VERSES

We are stewards, or managers, of the money and material things God has entrusted to us.

Reflect on the fact that God is the sole owner of *everything* as you consider the following Scriptures:

"The earth is the LORD's, and everything in it, the world, and all who live in it; for he founded it on the seas and established it on the waters" (Psalm 24:1–2).

"Everything in the heavens and earth is yours, O Lord, and this is your kingdom" (1 Chronicles 29:11 TLB).

God said, "Everything under heaven belongs to me" (Job 41:11).

"Listen, my people ... I am God, your God ... for every animal of the forest is mine, and the cattle on a thousand hills ... for the world is mine, and all that is in it" (Psalm 50:7, 10, 12).

"'The silver is mine and the gold is mine,' declares the LORD Almighty" (Haggai 2:8).

Note that when this verse was written, silver and gold were used as a form of currency, essentially money. So in effect, God is saying that *all money is His*.

Since the absolute biblical truth is that God owns everything, then logically, we are stewards or managers of the money and material things God has entrusted to us. We are not the owner. God is the owner!

Therefore, as stewards, we need to look to the owner, God, as to how we should manage His resources. If you believe you are the owner of the money and material wealth you possess, consider what you will think after you die. At that point, it will be evident that you were not an owner but merely a steward of the money and material things God gave you while here on earth.

In 1 Timothy 6:7, the apostle Paul said, "We brought nothing into the world, and we can take nothing out of it." Therefore, it is important to acknowledge God's ownership and learn and apply God's financial principles so you can fulfill your steward-ship responsibilities.

1. Definition of Christian Biblical Stewardship

To operate in Christian biblical stewardship means acknowledging—in mind and heart—that God owns everything. Secondly, it means using money and material things according to God's biblical principles and God's specific will for His designed purpose.

2. Our Stewardship Responsibilities

Let's begin with an understanding of our stewardship responsibilities and how to fulfill them:

- Spend quality time in prayer with the Lord regularly, asking God for His wisdom and direction in managing the money and material things He has entrusted to you. In James 1:5, God has promised, "If any of you lacks wisdom, you should ask God, who gives generously to all without finding fault, and it will be given to you."

  Further, Psalm 25:12 states, "Who, then, are those who fear the LORD? He will instruct them in the ways they should choose."

- With more than 2,300 references to money, the Bible offers plenty of financial wisdom. Therefore, study and meditate on God's word regularly concerning your finances. The Lord admonishes in Joshua 1:8, "Keep this Book of the Law always on your lips; meditate on it day and night, so that you may be careful to do everything written in it. Then you will be prosperous and successful."

- Manage your money according to God's specific will and trust God to provide for your needs. Proverbs 3:5–6, NKJV, reminds us, "Trust in the LORD with all your heart, and lean not on your own understanding; in all your ways submit to him, and he will make your paths straight."

3. God's Promises to Us and His Responsibilities

According to God's word, His promises and responsibilities to us include the following.

- God has promised to meet our needs if we put Him first. He reveals His desire to provide for us in Matthew 6:31–33:

  > "So do not worry, saying, 'What shall we eat?' or 'What shall we drink?' or 'What shall we wear?' For the pagans run after all these things, and your heavenly Father knows that you need them. But seek first his kingdom and his righteousness, and all these things will be given to you as well."

  Note that God has promised to meet our *needs*, but not necessarily our *wants* and *desires*. It's important to distinguish between the two as the Lord directs.

- God has promised to guide us in everything, including our financial decisions, according to His will. In Psalm 32:8, God said, "I will instruct you and teach you in the way you should go; I will counsel you with my loving eye on you." And accordingly, God's promise in Isaiah 58:11 says, "The LORD will guide you always."

Notice the relationship between our responsibilities and God's promises. As a steward, it is essential to understand the owner's instructions lest we misuse our resources. So as Christian stewards, we should *focus on God, His word, and His specific will.*

If we faithfully fulfill our stewardship responsibilities, we can completely trust God to direct our financial decisions and meet our needs regardless of our financial circumstances.

C. FIVE CRITICAL POINTS OF FINANCIAL STEWARDSHIP

1. Point #1: We Are All Individually Accountable to God

In the Parable of the Talents in Matthew 25:14–30, the master, God, entrusted different amounts of money to three servants, each according to their ability (this is true to life, as God does trust different people with varying amounts of income).

The servant with five talents gained five more, and the servant with two talents gained two more, while the servant with one talent buried his, *making no effort to invest* his master's money.

The praise God gave the servant who had five talents and earned five more was identical to the praise God gave the servant who had two talents and earned two more. That praise was "Well done, good and faithful servant. You have been faithful over a little; I will set you over much" (Matthew 25:23 ESV).

The vital point is that we are all individually accountable to God in managing the money He entrusts to us, regardless of how much we have or how much others have. Secondly, faithful stewardship will result in God's blessings and additional resources from the Lord.

2. Point #2: God Punishes Poor Stewardship

However, the lesson of the parable doesn't end there. Recall that the servant with one talent buried his and received no praise or blessing from the Lord. Many Christians are not aware that God's word is clear that God punishes poor stewardship. In Matthew 25:28–29, ESV, Jesus said:

"Take the talent from him and give it to the one who has the ten talents. For to everyone who has will more be given, and he will have an abundance. But from the one who has not, even what he has will be taken away."

This Scripture is often misunderstood because the words "to everyone who has" refers to everyone who has been a faithful steward by managing money God's way—then God will entrust them with more. However, "the one who has not" represents *unfaithful* servants whom God will punish by taking away whatever has been entrusted to them.

Therefore, let's choose to be faithful stewards of God's resources by acknowledging in our hearts and minds that God owns *everything*, and then by using money and material things according to God's financial principles and God's specific will.

3. Point #3: Everyone Is Accountable to the Lord, Not Just High-Income Earners

Often people believe they are not accountable to God because they don't have much money. This is not true. Romans 14:12 says, "So then, each of us will give an account of ourselves to God." In 1 Corinthians 4:2, we read, "Now it is required that those who have been given a trust must prove faithful."

The key is *faithfulness* to God. In other words, from God's perspective, it is not about how much money you have but whether or not you have been faithful to God and His word with the money and material things He has entrusted to you.

D. TWO QUESTIONS TO CONSIDER

Please contemplate the following questions and provide an answer:

1. Have you been managing money according to God's financial principles and specific will for your life? Explain why or why not.

_____

_____

_____

2. If you have *not* been managing money according to God's financial principles and specific will, what kind of a plan can you outline to get there?

_____

_____

_____

1. Point #4: God Provides Us with the Ability to Earn Income

It is common that when someone works hard to earn a good income, they assume they made it happen. Therefore, they may believe they are entitled to spend "their money" as they please.

But God's perspective is very different. Consider what the Lord said in Deuteronomy 8:17–18:

> "You may say to yourself, 'My power and the strength of my hands have produced this wealth for me.' But remember the LORD your God, for it is he who gives you the ability to produce wealth."

Further, 1 Corinthians 4:7 asks, "Who makes you different from anyone else? What do you have that you did not receive? And if you did receive it, why do you boast as though you did not?" And Ephesians 2:10 says, "For we are God's handiwork, created in Christ Jesus to do good works, which God prepared in advance for us to do."

As God's handiwork, we must acknowledge in our hearts and minds that God gave us our natural abilities, including the ability to earn a good income.

2. Point #5: You Don't Have to Be Wealthy to Be a Generous Giver

Some Christians believe they cannot give generously and will not receive significant rewards in heaven for their giving while on earth because their income is too low. This is false and unbiblical.

In the story of the widow's offering (see Luke 21), many wealthy people gave significant amounts into the temple treasury, while a poor widow put in two tiny copper coins. In other words, her contribution was insignificant in terms of monetary value. However, in light of her situation as a poor widow, Jesus didn't see it that way. Instead, Jesus said in Luke 21:3–4, "Truly I tell you, this poor widow has put in more than all the others. All these people gave their gifts out of their wealth; but she out of her poverty put in all she had to live on."

In other words, even if your income is modest, you should never feel that your contributions to the Lord are insignificant. Instead, God looks at the heart and assesses generous giving based on the biblical model of stewardship and management of all God has entrusted to you.

As for wealthy people, the Bible provides examples of godly people (like Abraham and Sarah, Abigail, David, and Job) to whom God entrusted significant wealth and who were also faithful stewards of God's resources.

Therefore, in summary, it is essential to demonstrate your faithfulness to God in managing the money and material things He has given you, regardless of your income level or degree of wealth.

E. MEMORY VERSES

Meditating upon God's word and committing it to memory enables you to think in a godly fashion with respect to managing the money and material things God has entrusted to you.

Recommended Memory Verses

- "Everything in the heavens and earth is yours, O Lord, and this is your kingdom. We adore you as being in control of everything. Riches and honor come from you alone, and you are the ruler of all mankind; your hand controls power and might, and it is at your discretion that men are made great and given strength" (1 Chronicles 29:11–12 TLB).

- "'The silver is mine and the gold is mine,' declares the LORD Almighty" (Haggai 2:8).

- "The earth is the LORD's, and everything in it, the world, and all who live in it; for he founded it on the seas and established it on the waters" (Psalm 24:1–2).

F. CASE STUDIES, QUESTIONS, TOM'S COMMENTS

1. Case Study #1: Two Brothers Manage Money Very Differently

Bill and Steve are brothers. Bill is married to Anne, and Steve is married to Marilyn. Both families earn a typical middle-class income.

Bill feels he has worked hard for his money and earned the right to spend it however he and his wife wish. They believe "you can't take it with you," so you might as well enjoy it now. As a result, Bill and Anne have no savings and are frequently "forced into debt" when an unexpected expenditure arises. Consequently, the couple has accumulated significant debt over the past few years. Therefore, phone calls from their creditors are commonplace in their home.

On the other hand, Steve and Marilyn are careful about spending their money. They are excellent at budgeting, ensuring all bills are paid on time, and willingly sacrifice to save more money. As a result, this couple feels secure, knowing they have ample savings and a substantial investment portfolio. By age 45, they have saved more than enough for their children's education and future retirement. Nevertheless, they continue to "pinch their pennies" to save even more.

However, it's not unusual for Steve and Marilyn to become anxious about their finances or lose sleep whenever their portfolio significantly decreases due to market volatility. Regarding giving, neither couple tithes regularly, gives offerings to the Lord's work, or is actively involved in ministry.

QUESTION #1

Do you feel that Bill and Anne practice biblical stewardship? See the definition above, and please explain your perspective.

_____

_____

_____

TOM'S COMMENT

No, Bill and Anne do not practice biblical stewardship, as they don't acknowledge God's ownership of the money God has entrusted to them. Instead, they believe they are the owners, and therefore, it is their right to spend as they wish—generally on selfish desires.

Further, Bill and Anne do not give the first fruits of their increase to God's work (Proverbs 3:9–10). In addition, they violate God's financial principles by spending more than they earn and accumulating debt (Proverbs 22:7). They are also a poor witness to their creditors as they do not pay their liabilities on time (Matthew 5:14–16).

QUESTION #2

Do you feel that Steve and Marilyn practice biblical stewardship? See the definition above, and please explain your perspective.

_____

_____

_____

TOM'S COMMENT

Steve and Marilyn apply some financial principles that are consistent with God's word, such as budgeting (Luke 14:28–30), paying bills on time (Romans 13:8), paying down debt (Proverbs 22:7), and saving for future needs, like their children's education and retirement (Proverbs 6:6–8).

Nevertheless, they do not *acknowledge in their hearts and minds that God owns everything.* Therefore, they do not give God their first fruits (Proverbs 3:9–10) and continue to save and accumulate when no longer necessary. In reality, despite what Steve and Marilyn may say, they trust their investments, not God (Luke 12:15–21).

QUESTION #3

What biblical financial principles have Bill and Anne violated? Please provide a Scripture reference for each point as able.

_____

_____

_____

TOM'S COMMENT

Bill and Anne have violated these biblical financial principles.

- Bill and Anne have no financial plan, like a budget (see Luke 14:28–30).

- They carry too much debt (see Proverbs 22:7).

- They do not pay their bills or creditors on time (see Romans 13:5; Matthew 5:14–16).

- They are selfish with their money (see Philippians 2:3–4).

- They focus on material things—"treasures on earth," rather than on things of eternal value—"treasures in heaven" (see Matthew 6:19–21).

- They spend all their income and have no savings (see Proverbs 21:20).

- They believe they are owners, not stewards (see 1 Chronicles 29:11–12).

- They do not give generously to God's work (see 2 Corinthians 9:6–7).

QUESTION #4

What biblical financial principles have Steve and Marilyn violated? Provide a Scripture reference for each point.

_____

_____

_____

TOM'S COMMENT

Steve and Marilyn have violated these biblical financial principles.

- Steve and Marilyn have a problem with hoarding money and trusting in their wealth rather than in God. This is the same problem demonstrated by "the rich fool" in Luke 12:15–21.

- They do not give generously to God's work (see 2 Corinthians 9:6–7).

• They have a problem desiring to get rich (see 1 Timothy 6:9–10).

QUESTION #5

Have Bill and Anne been a "spiritual light" to their creditors? In other words, do they have a good testimony as Christians to their creditors?

_____

_____

_____

TOM'S COMMENT

No, Bill and Anne do not have a good Christian testimony for their creditors because they neglect to pay their debts on time. In Matthew 5:16, Jesus said, "Let your light shine before others, that they may see your good deeds and glorify your Father in heaven."

Further, God instructs us in Romans 13:8, "Let no debt remain outstanding." So the critical question I raise is this: what kind of a light in a world of darkness is a Christian who does not pay their debts on time? The answer is that they are a poor witness for the Lord.

QUESTION #6

If both couples witnessed to their creditors, which couple do you think the creditors would be more likely to listen to?

_____

_____

_____

TOM'S COMMENT

The creditors would likely listen to Bill and Anne because they have paid their bills on time and have credibility in the eyes of their creditors (Matthew 5:14–16; Proverbs 3:27).

QUESTION #7

From a biblical perspective, what financial principles are Steve and Marilyn applying correctly? Please explain and give a reference to Scripture as able.

_____

_____

_____

TOM'S COMMENT

Steve and Marilyn have applied these biblical financial principles:

- Steve and Marilyn plan their finances well by implementing and following a budget (Luke 14:28–30; Proverbs 21:5).
- They pay their creditors on time (Matthew 5:14–16; Romans 13:8).
- They save for future needs (1 Timothy 5:8; Proverbs 21:20 TLB).
- They pay down their debt (Proverbs 22:7).

2. Scripture Application #1

Discuss the relevance and application of the following verses concerning Bill and Anne's situation.

"Do nothing out of selfish ambition or vain conceit. Rather, in humility value others above yourselves, not looking to your own interests but each of you to the interests of others" (Philippians 2:3–4).

_____

_____

_____

TOM'S COMMENT

Bill and Anne spend their money selfishly and ignore the interests of their creditors.

"You are the light of the world. A town built on a hill cannot be hidden. Neither do people light a lamp and put it under a bowl. Instead they put it on its stand, and it gives light to everyone in the house. In the same way, let your light shine before others, that they may see your good deeds and glorify your Father in heaven" (Matthew 5:14–16).

_____

_____

_____

TOM'S COMMENT

Bill and Anne need to understand that, as Christians, they are a terrible testimony to their creditors. Therefore, they will likely never be able to witness to their creditors since they are *not* a light in a world of darkness. But sadly, they are also a worldly example to their children with respect to the management of money.

Discuss the relevance and application of the following verses concerning Steve and Marilyn's situation.

"Though your riches increase, do not set your heart on them" (Psalm 62:10).

_____

_____

_____

_____

_____

TOM'S COMMENT

God instructed Steve and Marilyn that they should not "set their hearts" on their investments. From an eternal perspective, investing beyond one's future needs is meaningless, especially if the extra funds are withheld from building up God's kingdom (Matthew 6:19–21).

"Blessed is the one who trusts in the LORD, whose confidence is in him" (Jeremiah 17:7).

_____

_____

_____

_____

_____

TOM'S COMMENT

Steve and Marilyn need to learn to trust in God, not in their investment portfolio. If they do, they will be much happier and enjoy God's peace (John 14:27).

117

MANAGEMENT OF MONEY IMPACTS RELATIONSHIP WITH GOD, SPOUSE AND ETERNITY

"The plans of the diligent certainly lead to advantage, but everyone who is in a hurry certainly comes to poverty" (Proverbs 21:5 NASB).

_____

_____

_____

TOM'S COMMENT

To their credit, Steve and Marilyn have diligently saved, invested, and paid down debt. They have not made any hasty financial decisions. By following God's biblical principles, they are much better off financially than Bill and Anne. However, they fall short in that they need to set their minds on things above (Colossians 3:1–2) and start investing money into God's work, which will result in eternal rewards (Acts 20:35).

3. Case Study #2: A Couple Manages Money God's Way, and God Blesses Them Abundantly!

Ron and Marion are a married couple. Shortly after becoming Christians, they felt led by the Lord to learn what God's word said about finances. In addition to reading God's word regularly, they read Christian books on money management written by Larry Burkett and Howard Dayton.

They first learn about the biblical principle of stewardship, that they are stewards or managers of the money and material possessions God entrusted to them, and that God was the owner. This revelation changes their spending habits. As a result, they prayerfully seek God's will before making any major financial decisions. Even when they can afford to pay cash for something, they ask God in prayer what they should do with His money.

Although Ron's business is small, they demonstrate their trust in God by tithing faithfully. Ron and Marion also understand that God warns of the dangers of debt and discourages debt. Therefore, they are motivated to diligently work hard to pay off their personal and business loans.

Today, they are entirely debt-free, both personally and corporately! As they continue to learn and apply God's financial principles in managing their finances, God blesses Ron's business. Today, Ron has a successful business that enables him and Marion to give generously to the Lord's work, way beyond 10 per cent!

Ron acknowledges God's blessings of a profitable business and the ability to earn a substantial income. Nevertheless, Ron and Marion feel led by the Lord to continue living in their quaint middle-class home and driving used cars. Ron is not bothered that most of his business associates have more impressive vehicles, while Marion is satisfied with her home. They both desire to store up "treasures in heaven" that will last for eternity.

4. Review the Definition of Biblical Stewardship

To operate in Christian biblical stewardship means acknowledging—in mind and heart—that God owns *everything*. Secondly, to use money and material things according to God's biblical principles and God's specific will for His designed purpose.

QUESTION #1

Given this definition, do Ron and Marion practice faithful biblical stewardship?

_____

_____

_____

_____

_____

_____

TOM'S COMMENT

Yes, Ron and Marion practice biblical stewardship as demonstrated by:

- They acknowledge that God owns all of their money and material things (Haggai 2:8), including Ron's business, and they are merely the stewards or managers (Matthew 25:14–30).

- They have learned and implemented biblical financial principles, such as contentment (Luke 3:10), giving generously (2 Corinthians 9:6–7), and debt reduction (Proverbs 22:7).

- They are careful to follow God's will. In other words, they will not make any major purchases until they have a clear directive from God (Psalm 32:8), even when they have the money (Luke 22:42).

QUESTION #2

When their income was modest, Ron and Marion had the mind-set of stewards, not owners, with regard to the money God had entrusted to them. Do you think this attitude was critical in determining how they would handle a large surplus?

_____

_____

_____

TOM'S COMMENT

Yes, absolutely! A person's management of money is determined by one's attitude or mindset toward money, which will generally rule regardless of the amount of income. That's why Jesus said that if you are not trustworthy with a small amount, you will not be trustworthy with a large amount (Luke 16:10).

In many ways, one's management of money is a reflection of one's character and priorities, which generally do not change as one's income changes.

QUESTION #3

How would you describe Ron and Marion's *attitude* regarding the lifestyle God had ordained for them? Is this consistent with biblical principles? Please explain your answer, and provide a reference to Scripture.

_____

_____

_____

TOM'S COMMENT

Ron and Marion's attitude concerning their lifestyle is that of contentment, which is consistent with biblical principles (Philippians 4:11–13; 1 Timothy 6:6–8). Contentment may be the most essential godly attitude toward money and material things. I sincerely believe that *contentment is the "antidote" to many worldly attitudes, such as selfishness, covetousness, envy, and greed.*

Hebrews 13:5 says, "Keep your lives free from the love of money and be content with what you have, because God has said, 'Never will I leave you; never will I forsake you.'"

QUESTION #4

Would it be wrong for Ron and Marion to purchase a more expensive home, which they could easily afford?

_____

_____

_____

TOM'S COMMENT

Generally speaking, it is not wrong for a Christian to own a bigger home if it is within their budget and consistent with God's will for their life. However, every Christian must ensure they live within God's will regarding their personal lifestyle and not purchase something simply because it is affordable or on sale. In this case, Ron and Marion discern the will of the Lord and live within the will of God for their lives.

I've provided biblical counsel to thousands of financially successful people since 1982, and I have observed that unfortunately, most people "raise their standard of living" rather than "raise their standard of giving" when their income increases. From my experience, only a small percentage of Christians can be trusted with large amounts of money, as most will spend it on themselves.

Sadly, most Christians do not have an eternal perspective when it comes to money and material things (Colossians 3:1–2; Matthew 6:19–21; 19:29).

5. Scripture Application #2

Discuss the relevance and application of the following verses concerning Ron and Marion's situation; then write your comments for each verse.

> "Remember this: Whoever sows sparingly will also reap sparingly, and whoever sows generously will also reap generously. Each of you should give what you have decided in your heart to give, not reluctantly or under compulsion, for God loves a cheerful giver" (2 Corinthians 9:6–7).

_____

_____

_____

TOM'S COMMENT

Ron and Marion gave generously, and God blessed them with significant income and material wealth. Please note what it says a few verses later, in 2 Corinthians 9:10–11:

> "Now he who supplies seed to the sower and bread for food will also supply and increase your store of seed and will enlarge the harvest of your righteousness. You will be enriched in every way so that you can be generous on every occasion, and through us your generosity will result in thanksgiving to God."

"Whoever can be trusted with very little can also be trusted with much, and whoever is dishonest with very little will also be dishonest with much" (Luke 16:10).

_____

_____

_____

TOM'S COMMENT

Ron and Marion were trustworthy with a modest income and therefore are trustworthy with a more significant income. This is because they apply biblical principles and godly attitudes toward money regardless of income level.

Hence, if an individual mismanages a small amount of money, Jesus predicts they will mismanage a considerable amount. In other words, one will apply the same *worldly mindset and attitude* to managing a higher income as with a lower income.

"Do not store up for yourselves treasures on earth, where moths and vermin destroy, and where thieves break in and steal. But store up for yourselves treasures in heaven, where moths and vermin do not destroy, and where thieves do not break in and steal. For where your treasure is, there your heart will be also" (Matthew 6:19–21).

_____

_____

_____

TOM'S COMMENT

Ron and Marion store up "treasures in heaven" by giving generously to God's work and being content with a middle-class lifestyle beneath their means. The way they manage their money according to biblical principles is a godly example to their friends, relatives, creditors, and business associates. Furthermore, it is an excellent example for their children.

Their faithful stewardship of the money and material things God has entrusted to them will result in treasures in heaven. And when they reach heaven, they will receive eternal rewards for their faithfulness (see the parable of the ten minas in Luke 19:11–27 and Matthew 16:27).

"Remember the LORD your God, for it is he who gives you the ability to produce wealth, and so confirms his covenant, which he swore to your ancestors, as it is today" (Deuteronomy 8:18).

_____

_____

_____

TOM'S COMMENT

Ron acknowledges that God gave him the ability to manage a profitable business. Because of his godly attitude, Ron regularly asks God to direct him on utilizing the money God entrusts to him. He remains humble and reliant on the Lord, as his high income has not resulted in pride, which is typical for prosperous people, including financially successful Christians. James 4:6 says, "God opposes the proud but shows favor to the humble."

125

"This is what I have observed to be good: that it is appropriate for a person to eat, to drink and to find satisfaction in their toilsome labor under the sun during the few days of life God has given them—for this is their lot. Moreover, when God gives someone wealth and possessions, and the ability to enjoy them, to accept their lot and be happy in their toil—this is a gift of God" (Ecclesiastes 5:18–19).

_____

_____

_____

TOM'S COMMENT

Despite their ability to buy a bigger home and more expensive vehicles, Ron and Marion enjoy the wealth and possessions God has given them. Their contentment is a gift from God. Furthermore, they have no debt. Instead, they have a significant surplus. As such, they experience God's peace in their finances. Therefore, if the Lord directs them to enjoy more of their wealth, they should do so as He leads, without any guilt.

6. Case Study #3: A Couple with a Modest Income Are Faithful Stewards Whom God Blesses in Unusual Ways

John and Carol are married with four children. John earns a below-average salary, and Carol is a stay-at-home mom because caring for their four children is a full-time job. Considering their large family and only one modest income, their cash flow is tight. As a result, John and Carol budget carefully and spend their money wisely.

The couple learned from studying relevant Scriptures on finances that tithing is a tangible way to demonstrate their absolute commitment to God and trust in Him. Therefore, although challenging, they faithfully give 10 per cent of their income to the Lord's work.

John and Carol also acknowledge God's blessings of good health, a happy marriage, and four children who have all accepted Jesus Christ as their Saviour and Lord. In addition to leading their children to Christ, they have been privileged to lead other relatives and friends to the Lord, which they see as a great blessing.

The couple believes that everything they own belongs to God, and they are managers of what He has entrusted to them— their home, all their income, and even their children. Although their income is modest, they believe they must be good stewards in managing the money and material things God has provided them.

Whenever they have a material need, John and Carol sincerely pray to the Lord, asking for God's wisdom, direction, and provision. They often see God provide in unusual ways—sometimes with a "little miracle," such as unexpected money, a gift from a friend, or an incredible deal on a purchase. John and Carol have learned to trust God to meet their needs as they put Him first in every area of their lives.

QUESTION #1

Have John and Carol practiced biblical stewardship? Please review my previous definition and explain your perspective.

_____

_____

_____

TOM'S COMMENT

Yes, John and Carol have practiced biblical stewardship as demonstrated by the following:

- They acknowledge that their home, income, and even their children belong to God; that they are managers of everything God has entrusted to them (Psalm 24:1–2).

- They have a godly attitude (contentment) with respect to money and apply biblical principles, such as budgeting, tithing, and trusting God to meet their needs (Proverbs 3:5–6).

- They put God first (Matthew 6:31–33), as demonstrated by giving the first 10 per cent of their increase to the Lord, notwithstanding their modest income.

QUESTION #2

How would you describe their attitude toward money and material things? Please explain your answer.

_____

_____

_____

TOM'S COMMENT

John and Carol demonstrate that "godliness with contentment is great gain" (1 Timothy 6:6–8), as they are content with having their basic needs met.

Their focus is on things of greater importance than money, like leading their children, friends, and relatives to Jesus Christ (Colossians 3:1–2). They understand that they are stewards, not owners of the money, material things, and everything God has given them. Thus, they are faithful stewards of the Lord's resources (1 Corinthians 4:2).

QUESTION #3

What impact will John and Carol's management of money likely have upon their children?

_____

_____

_____

TOM'S COMMENT

John and Carol are a godly example of biblical stewardship, so the impact on their children will be very positive. Their children will likely adopt the same stewardship mindset regarding money and material things, including tithing and being content with God's provision. Proverbs 22:6 says, "Train up a child in the way he should go; even when he is old he will not depart from it" (ESV).

QUESTION #4

In what ways has God blessed John and Carol?

_____

_____

_____

TOM'S COMMENT

Here are some of the ways God has blessed John and Carol:

- They have four children who have a personal relationship with Jesus Christ, and their future grandchildren will also likely know the Lord.

- They have a wonderful marriage and experience contentment as well as God's peace (most people do not have the peace of God in their finances because they violate biblical principles and are not content).

- They have been privileged to lead their children, as well as several friends and relatives, to Christ. An individual's salvation is a "treasure in heaven" that will last for eternity (Matthew 6:19–21), and nothing is more significant than that.

QUESTION #5

Do you think John and Carol's impact on their four children and others has anything to do with their godly money management? Please explain your view, and provide a reference to Scripture for each point.

_____

_____

TOM'S COMMENT

Yes, John and Carol's biblical money management is a light in a world of darkness (Matthew 5:14–16) and a godly testimony for their children, friends, and relatives. At times, God's blessings for biblical stewardship are non-monetary, such as the gift of godly children, a happy marriage, good health, and "the peace of God, which transcends all understanding" (Philippians 4:4–7).

7. Scripture Application #3

Discuss the relevance and application of the following verses concerning John and Carol's situation. Write your comments for each verse.

"Godliness with contentment is great gain. For we brought nothing into the world, and we can take nothing out of it. But if we have food and clothing, we will be content with that" (1 Timothy 6:6–8).

_____

_____

_____

_____

_____

_____

TOM'S COMMENT

John and Carol exemplify the godly characteristics mentioned in these verses—specifically godliness and contentment. God desires these virtues to be key priorities in our lives.

"It is required that those who have been given a trust must prove faithful" (1 Corinthians 4:2).

_____

_____

_____

_____

_____

TOM'S COMMENT

God requires faithfulness regardless of the amount of money He entrusts to you. John and Carol have demonstrated faithfulness even with their modest income.

"If the willingness is there, the gift is acceptable according to what one has, not according to what one does not have" (2 Corinthians 8:12).

_____

_____

_____

_____

_____

TOM'S COMMENT

God evaluates and blesses our giving in light of our income. Giving 10 per cent of a modest income requires much more faith and sacrifice than giving 10 percent of a high income. God understands the difference and blesses accordingly here on earth and in eternity (Matthew 19:29).

"Do not set your heart on what you will eat or drink; do not worry about It. For the pagan world runs after all such things, and your Father knows that you need them. But seek his kingdom, and these things will be given to you as well" (Luke 12:29–31).

_____

_____

_____

_____

_____

TOM'S COMMENT

John and Carol put God first in every aspect of their lives, including their finances. As a result, God fulfilled His promise to meet their every need.

8. Pray About and Meditate Upon God's Will for Your Finances

In Proverbs 21:1, we read, "In the LORD's hand the king's heart is a stream of water that he channels toward all who please him." If God can direct the heart of a king, He can certainly direct your heart.

With that in mind, I encourage you to spend at least ten minutes in prayer to ask God by His Spirit to direct your heart and mind to genuinely believe He owns everything, and to help you understand that you are only stewarding and managing His resources and what He has provided for you.

As you reflect, pray once more and ask the Lord to reveal several practical ways to help you acknowledge that He owns everything and that you are merely a steward and manager of the money and material possessions He has entrusted to you.

List as many as you can, and provide a Scripture reference for each.

_____

_____

_____

TOM'S COMMENT

Here are some ideas to help you acknowledge in your heart and mind that God owns everything and that you are a steward of His resources:

- Meditate on and memorize relevant Scriptures (Joshua 1:8) that emphasize God's ownership of money and material things, such as 1 Chronicles 29:11–12, Psalm 24:1–2, and Haggai 2:8.

- Praise God and thank Him often for how He has blessed you (Psalm 118:1).

- Before making any significant financial decision, spend time in prayer, listening for God's voice (John 10:27) and discerning God's specific direction (Psalm 32:8). Be prepared to act according to the will of God, not your will (Luke 22:42).

- Practice using possessive nouns. For example, say "God's home" (not my home), "God's car," "God's business," and "God's money."

- Give generously to God's work (2 Corinthians 9:6–7). You cannot be selfish and generous at the same time!

- Make your relationship with God a priority by enjoying your fellowship with Him. If you "take delight in the LORD," then He will "give you the desires of your heart," which are His desires for you (Psalm 37:4).

• Develop and maintain a close personal relationship with the Lord Jesus Christ, utterly dependent upon Him at all times. Recall Jesus's words in John 15:5–8:

"I am the vine; you are the branches. If you remain in me and I in you, you will bear much fruit; apart from me you can do nothing. If you do not remain in me, you are like a branch that is thrown away and withers; such branches are picked up, thrown into the fire and burned. If you remain in me and my words remain in you, ask whatever you wish, and it will be done for you. This is to my Father's glory, that you bear much fruit, showing yourselves to be my disciples."

9. Summary of God's Promises and Our Stewardship Responsibilities

The most essential and foundational biblical financial principle for us to fully understand and acknowledge in our hearts and minds, even deep into our souls, is that *everything we have comes from God.* This includes the time, talents, money, and material things God has provided to us.

In other words, God owns everything we have, and we are merely His stewards and managers. As a result, we must regularly look to the owner and His word to determine how we should manage the money and material things He has entrusted us (review the parable of the talents in Matthew 25:14–30).

Therefore, before making any significant financial decisions, or even as you make minor financial decisions, ask the Lord to direct you (Psalm 25:12) as to what you should do with His money (Haggai 2:8). Use God's money according to His specific will, not to satisfy your own wants and desires (Luke 22:42).

Remember, if indeed you manage money God's way, when you stand before the Lord at "the judgment seat of Christ" (2 Corinthians 5:10), you will hear the very words you long to hear: "Well done, good and faithful servant! You have been faithful with a few things; I will put you in charge of many things. Come and share in your master's happiness!" (Matthew 25:21).

A part of sharing in the master's happiness is enjoying eternal rewards in heaven for having invested God's money according to His financial principles and specific will. In Matthew 16:27, Jesus said, "The Son of Man is going to come in his Father's glory with his angels, and then he will reward each person according to what they have done."

IV.

DEVELOPING GODLY ATTITUDES TOWARD MONEY

A. OBJECTIVE OF THIS CHAPTER

To learn how to develop godly attitudes toward money and material things.

B. KEY BIBLICAL PRINCIPLE

God's word distinguishes between godly attitudes and motives toward money and material things and worldly attitudes and motives toward money and material things. As Christians, we are admonished to have godly attitudes and motives toward money and material things.

1. Overview of Godly and Worldly Attitudes Toward Money

As a matter of substance, money is neither moral nor immoral. There is no spiritual aspect to money, nor is it unspiritual. In other words, money is neutral, as there is nothing inherently good or bad about money in and of itself.

You can use money to advance God's kingdom, or you can use it for purposes contrary to God's word. Either way, God reveals His concern about our attitudes and motives toward money. For example, in 1 Timothy 6:9–10, the apostle Paul warns of the dangers of the "love of money":

"Those who want to get rich fall into temptation and a trap and into many foolish and harmful desires that plunge people into ruin and destruction. For the love of money is a root of all kinds of evil. Some people, eager for money, have wandered from the faith and pierced themselves with many griefs."

The root of all kinds of evil is not money. It is the "love of money" that is a root of all kinds of evil. The love of money is a worldly attitude that, if allowed to develop, will lead you down a destructive path. Consequently, it can destroy you and your family physically, emotionally, and spiritually.

2. Some Indicators of the Love of Money

The following are some indicators of the love of money, although this is not an exhaustive list:

- Working excessively hard (Proverbs 23:4–5).

- Spending little to no time with God daily (John 10:27).

- Having minimal or no ministry involvement (Ephesians 2:10).

- Giving little or neglecting to give tithes and offerings to God's work (Proverbs 3:9–10).

- Living a selfish or lavish lifestyle without a desire to seek God's will for your life (see the parable of the rich fool in Luke 12:13–21).

Regardless of how much money and material possessions you accumulate, the attitude of the love of money will never be satisfied. According to Ecclesiastes 5:10, "Whoever loves money never has enough; whoever loves wealth is never satisfied with their income."

Other worldly attitudes include covetousness, lack of contentment, greed, selfishness, and pride. If any of these dominate your thinking, the consequences can be detrimental. On the other hand, godly attitudes toward money and material things include contentment, generosity, unselfishness, thankfulness to God, and humility.

3. Wealthy Christians versus Those Who Have Little Money

It is not wrong for a Christian to have a lot of money and own nice things. Abraham, Sarah, David, Abigail, and Job are examples of godly people to whom God entrusted significant wealth. However, these great people of faith used the material wealth God provided according to God's will for His honor and glory. Put another way, their godly attitudes toward money produced actions consistent with God's word and His will.

I know of several successful entrepreneurs who demonstrate godly attitudes toward money. In their hearts and minds, they acknowledge God's ownership of everything they have, including their businesses.

As committed believers, they use the money God has entrusted to them according to His will and not their own. Further, they often give much of their income to God's work and utilize their business resources for Christian ministry.

Similarly, many people with modest incomes have godly attitudes toward money. They are content with God's provision and focus on things of eternal value, such as evangelism and ministry, rather than on things of temporal value, such as material things (Matthew 6:19–21).

So the most important thing is not the amount of money you have, but *your attitude toward it*—and your attitude or mindset towards money and material things will determine how you use those resources.

Apart from a *close personal relationship with Jesus Christ*, anyone can struggle with covetousness, selfishness, greed, or other worldly attitudes.

When a Christian struggles with worldly attitudes toward money, God's word reveals the underlying cause to be a spiritual struggle between our sinful nature and God's Holy Spirit. In Galatians 5:16–18, the apostle Paul instructs:

"Walk by the Spirit, and you will not gratify the desires of the flesh. For the flesh desires what is contrary to the Spirit, and the Spirit what is contrary to the flesh. They are in conflict with each other, so that you are not to do whatever you want. But if you are led by the Spirit, you are not under the law."

Paul had to learn contentment and realize that only God could enable one to be content with His provision. Philippians 4:11–13 gives us a glimpse into Paul's heart on this matter:

"I am not saying this because I am in need, for I have learned to be content whatever the circumstances. I know what it is to be in need, and I know what it is to have plenty. I have learned the secret of being content in any and every situation, whether well fed or hungry, whether living in plenty or in want. I can do all this through him who gives me strength."

If you strive to overcome an ungodly and worldly attitude toward money on your own, you will likely have little success. However, if you depend on the Lord (John 15:5), pray for strength (Philippians 4:13) and wisdom (James 1:5), and focus on things of eternal value rather than temporal things (Colossians 3:1–2), I believe God will answer your prayer. I say this with complete confidence in the authority of God's word.

Toward the end of this chapter, you will find some practical ideas to help you overcome a worldly attitude. One doesn't have to look far to see that most Christians struggle with one or more worldly attitudes toward money and material things, resulting in financial difficulties.

Since 1982, I have been privileged to counsel more than twenty thousand individuals and couples with their personal finances. In most cases, I found those with serious financial difficulties had a worldly attitude toward money and material things as the underlying cause of their financial problems. Examples of this will be provided through case studies later in this chapter.

4. The Importance of Meditating on God's Word

It is necessary to meditate on God's word to change a worldly attitude or mindset concerning money into a godly one (Joshua 1:8) because God's word is powerful. Hebrews 4:12–13 states:

> "The word of God is alive and active. Sharper than any double-edged sword, it penetrates even to dividing soul and spirit, joints and marrow; it judges the thoughts and attitudes of the heart. Nothing in all creation is hidden from God's sight. Everything is uncovered and laid bare before the eyes of him to whom we must give account."

141

C. RECOMMENDED MEMORY VERSES

I encourage you to meditate on the following Scriptures to change how you think about and manage money and material things (Romans 12:2).

"Not that I speak from need, for I have learned to be content in whatever circumstances I am. I know how to get along with little, and I also know how-to live-in prosperity; in any and every circumstance I have learned the secret of being filled and going hungry, both of having abundance and suffering need. I can do all things through Him who strengthens me" (Philippians 4:11–13 NASB).

"Whoever loves money never has enough; whoever loves wealth is never satisfied with their income" (Ecclesiastes 5:10).

1. Distinguishing between Worldly and Godly Attitudes Toward Money

To develop and maintain a godly attitude or a godly mindset toward money, you must be able to distinguish between a godly attitude and a worldly attitude.

To help you in this process, I created the following chart. I recommend you prayerfully read through these comparisons and ask God to speak to you through His word (Psalm 119:105) and His Spirit (John 10:27) about the areas you need to improve.

I encourage you to pray as David prayed in Psalm 139:23–24: "Search me, God, and know my heart; test me and know my anxious thoughts. See if there is any offensive way in me, and lead me in the way everlasting."

D. CHART: WORLDLY ATTITUDES VERSUS GODLY ATTITUDES

WORLDLY ATTITUDE	GODLY ATTITUDE
1. Trusting in money and material things	**1. Trusting solely in God at all times and in all circumstances**
In the parable of the rich fool, Jesus called the rich man a fool because he trusted in his money and material things, not in God (Luke 12:13–21).	"Trust in the Lord with all your heart, and lean not on your own understanding; in all your ways acknowledge Him, and He shall direct your paths" (Proverbs 3:5–6 NKJV).
2. Believing money and material things bring happiness and peace of mind	**2. Believing true happiness and peace are only obtained through a close relationship with Jesus Christ**
In explaining the parable of the sower, Jesus said, "The seed falling among the thorns refers to someone who hears the word, but the worries of this life and the deceitfulness of wealth choke the word, making it un-fruitful" (Matthew 13:22).	"Peace I leave with you; my peace I give you. I do not give to you as the world gives. Do not let your hearts be troubled and do not be afraid" (John 14:27).

143

WORLDLY ATTITUDE	GODLY ATTITUDE
3. Having a strong desire for riches	**3. Being content with God's provision**
"Do not wear yourself out to get rich; do not trust your own cleverness. Cast but a glance at riches, and they are gone, for they will surely sprout wings and fly off to the sky like an eagle" (Proverbs 23:4–5).	"Godliness with contentment is great gain. For we brought nothing into the world, and we can take nothing out of it. But if we have food and clothing, we will be content with that" (1 Timothy 6:6–8).
4. Serving money	**4. Serving God**
"No one can serve two masters. Either you will hate the one and love the other, or you will be devoted to the one and despise the other. You cannot serve both God and money" (Matthew 6:24).	"The people said to Joshua, 'We will serve the Lord our God and obey him'" (Joshua 24:24).
5. Being prideful	**5. Being humble**
"God opposes the proud but shows favor to the humble" (James 4:6).	"Humble yourselves before the Lord, and he will lift you up" (James 4:10).

WORLDLY ATTITUDE	GODLY ATTITUDE
6. Believing you are independent of God	**6. Acknowledging your complete dependency on God**
"You may say to yourself, 'My power and the strength of my hands have produced this wealth for me.' But remember the Lord your God, for it is he who gives you the ability to produce wealth" (Deuteronomy 8:17–18).	Jesus said, "I am the vine; you are the branches. If you remain in me and I in you, you will bear much fruit; apart from me you can do nothing" (John 15:5).
7. Treasuring money and material things	**7. Treasuring things of eternal value**
"Do not store up for yourselves treasures on earth, where moths and vermin destroy, and where thieves break in and steal. But store up for yourselves treasures in heaven, where moths and vermin do not destroy, and where thieves do not break in and steal. For where your treasure is, there your heart will be also" (Matthew 6:19–21).	"Since, then, you have been raised with Christ, set your hearts on things above, where Christ is, seated at the right hand of God. Set your minds on things above, not on earthly things" (Colossians 3:1–2).

145

WORLDLY ATTITUDE	GODLY ATTITUDE
8. Being greedy	**8. Giving generously**
"Watch out! Be on your guard against all kinds of greed; life does not consist in an abundance of possessions" (Luke 12:15).	"Give, and it will be given to you. A good measure, pressed down, shaken together and running over, will be poured into your lap. For with the measure you use, it will be measured to you" (Luke 6:38).
9. Being covetous	**9. Being content**
"You shall not covet your neighbor's house. You shall not covet your neighbor's wife, or his male or female servant, his ox or donkey, or anything that belongs to your neighbor" (Exodus 20:17).	"I am not saying this because I am in need, for I have learned to be content whatever the circumstances. I know what it is to be in need, and I know what it is to have plenty. I have learned the secret of being content in any and every situation, whether well fed or hungry, whether living in plenty or in want. I can do all this through him who gives me strength" (Philippians 4:11–13).

WORLDLY ATTITUDE	GODLY ATTITUDE
10. Worrying excessively about money problems	**10. Trusting God to meet your needs**
"Do not worry, saying, 'What shall we eat?' or 'What shall we drink?' or 'What shall we wear' For the pagans run after all these things, and your heavenly Father knows that you need them. But seek first his kingdom and his righteousness, and all these things will be given to you as well" (Matthew 6:31–33).	"My God will meet all your needs according to the riches of his glory in Christ Jesus" (Philippians 4:19).
11. Loving money and material things	**11. Loving God**
"Keep your lives free from the love of money and be content with what you have, because God has said, 'Never will I leave you; never will I forsake you'" (Hebrews13:5).	"Jesus replied, 'Love the Lord your God with all your heart and with all your soul and with all your mind.' This is the first and greatest commandment" (Matthew 22:37–38).

WORLDLY ATTITUDE	GODLY ATTITUDE
12. Being ungrateful and complaining about your income and possessions	12. Being grateful and thankful for God's provision of your income and possessions

"Whoever loves money never has enough; whoever loves wealth is never satisfied with their income" (Ecclesiastes 5:10).

"The Lord said to Moses and Aaron: 'How long will this wicked community grumble against me? I have heard the complaints of these grumbling Israelites. So tell them, "As surely as I live, declares the Lord, I will do to you the very things I heard you say: In this wilderness your bodies will fall—every one of you twenty years old or more who was counted in the census and who has grumbled against me. Not one of you will enter the land I swore with uplifted hand to make your home, except Caleb son of Jephunneh and Joshua son of Nun""" (Numbers 14:26–30).

"Let them give thanks to the Lord for his unfailing love and his wonderful deeds for mankind, for he satisfies the thirsty and fills the hungry with good things" (Psalm 107:8–9).

"Give thanks to the Lord, for he is good; his love endures forever" (Psalm 118:1).

E. CASE STUDIES, QUESTIONS, TOM'S COMMENTS

1. Case Study #1: A Married Couple Lacks Contentment

Robert and Elizabeth are married with two children. Robert works full-time and earns an above-average income, while Elizabeth works part-time. They are both unhappy with their present income level and would like to increase it substantially. As a result, Robert is looking for a part-time job to supplement his full-time income, and Elizabeth is looking for full-time work.

The couple often talks about the more luxurious lives of some of their friends and relatives. Even though they already have an expensive lifestyle, they want more. For example, Robert owns an excellent vehicle typical of a middle-class income earner, yet he would like a more expensive car, like the one his friend Jack owns. On the other hand, Elizabeth desires a larger and more stately home, even though their current home meets their needs. This couple believes they will be happy once they acquire the upgrades and possessions they want.

Robert and Elizabeth often feel inferior in comparison to others who enjoy higher income levels, nicer homes, and more expensive things. To present and maintain an image of success, they often buy things they don't need, generally on credit. Thus, in addition to a large mortgage, they accumulate substantial debt, max out their credit cards, and reach the limit on their line of credit.

Consequently, they spend more than they earn, thus accumulating a greater debt load each month. Not surprisingly, the couple often receives calls from their bank and creditors pressuring them for overdue loan payments.

Because of their excess debt, they often argue about finances, which is destroying their marriage relationship. If it continues, separation, and eventually divorce, will likely be the result.

In the following questions, please reflect on the case study, write your answers, and provide a reference to Scripture for each point you have. Try not to look at Tom's answers until you have given each question some thought.

QUESTION #1

What would you consider to be the underlying causes of Robert and Elizabeth's financial problems?

_____

_____

_____

_____

_____

_____

TOM'S COMMENT

Robert and Elizabeth have adopted several worldly attitudes toward money and material things, causing them to make financial decisions that are inconsistent with God's word.

At a deeper level, they have *a spiritual problem* in that they do not think the way God thinks about money and material things. Instead, their worldly mindset concerning money and material things dominates how they manage their finances, which is contrary to God's word. They may not realize this since they have not studied what the Bible says about finances. God's word, the Bible, provides the absolute truth concerning how we are to manage money. In John 17:17, Jesus said, "Sanctify them by the truth; your word is truth."

QUESTION #2

What worldly attitudes do Robert and Elizabeth struggle with? Please provide a Scripture reference for each point.

_____

_____

_____

_____

_____

_____

_____

_____

_____

TOM'S COMMENT

Here is a list of the worldly attitudes Robert and Elizabeth struggle with.

- Robert and Elizabeth believe that money and material things will bring happiness. They fall into the same category as "The seed that fell among thorns" (Luke 8:14), for whom "the worries of this life and the deceitfulness of wealth choke the word, making it unfruitful" (Matthew 13:22).

- Their worldly attitude and mindset to make more money to acquire more possessions make them *spiritually unfruitful.* In 1 Timothy 6:10, the apostle Paul warns, "The love of money is a root of all kinds of evil. Some people, eager for money, have wandered from the faith and pierced themselves with many griefs."

- They have a worldly desire to get rich. Proverbs 23:4–5 states, "Do not wear yourself out to get rich; do not trust your own cleverness. Cast but a glance at riches, and they are gone, for they will surely sprout wings and fly off to the sky like an eagle."

- They serve money and material things rather than God. Jesus said, "No one can serve two masters. Either you will hate the one and love the other, or you will be devoted to the one and despise the other. You cannot serve both God and money" (Matthew 6:24).

- They treasure money and material things (Matthew 6:19–21) more than their relationship with God and things of eternal value. In Colossians 3:2, Paul instructs, "Set your mind on things above, not on earthly things."

- They covet what others have. Exodus 20:17 is one commandment where God warns, "You shall not covet your neighbor's house. You shall not covet your neighbor's wife, or his male or female servant, his ox or donkey, or anything that belongs to your neighbor."

- They are greedy and selfish. In Luke 12:15, Christ warned, "Watch out! Be on your guard against all kinds of greed; life does not consist in an abundance of possessions."

- They love money and material things. Hebrews 13:5 admonishes, "Keep your lives free from the love of money and be content with what you have, because God has said, 'Never will I leave you; never will I forsake you.'"

- They lack contentment in their thinking. The apostle Paul had to learn contentment, and we must do likewise (Philippians 4:11–13). Further, John the Baptist said, "Be content with your pay" (Luke 3:14).

- They are ungrateful for God's provision and complain, instead of expressing gratitude to God for their many blessings. Psalm 107:8–9 states, "Let them give thanks to the LORD for his unfailing love and his wonderful deeds for mankind, for he satisfies the thirsty and fills the hungry with good things."

QUESTION #3

Robert and Elizabeth often feel inferior to others with a higher income. Does God see them this way? What advice would you give them in this regard? Before reading Tom's comments and suggested solutions, write your answer and provide a Scripture reference for each point.

_____

_____

_____

_____

_____

_____

TOM'S COMMENT

In the eyes of God, it doesn't matter what Robert and Elizabeth have or do not have in terms of money and material possessions. It is important to remember that "The LORD does not see as man sees; for man looks at the outward appearance, but the LORD looks at the heart (1 Samuel 16:7 NKJV).

Further, because God is in control (Psalm 103:19), He determines their level of income and prosperity. First Chronicles 29:11–12 states,

> "Everything in the heavens and earth is yours, O Lord, and this is your kingdom. We adore you as being in control of everything. Riches and honor come from you alone, and you are the ruler of all mankind; your hand controls power and might, and it is at your discretion that men are made great and given strength" (TLB).

Moreover, Robert and Elizabeth need to humble themselves before the Lord and learn to be content with His provision (Luke 3:14). In addition, their focus must shift from things of temporal value, such as money and material things (Mark 8:36), to things of eternal value (Matthew 6:19–21). If they learn and apply God's financial principles in His word, God will provide for their every need (Matthew 6:31–33), but not necessarily their wants and desires.

QUESTION #4

Do you think Robert and Elizabeth would be content and happy if they achieved their desire for a significantly higher income? Explain your answer, and provide a reference to Scripture if able.

_____

_____

_____

TOM'S COMMENT

Robert and Elizabeth may experience superficial happiness in the short term, but they will not find true happiness in the long run. The reason is revealed in Ecclesiastes 5:10, where

God warns, "Whoever loves money never has money enough; whoever loves wealth is never satisfied with his income."

QUESTION #5

What biblically-based financial advice would you provide Robert and Elizabeth if you were their financial adviser? Provide a Scripture reference for each point to ensure your counsel is biblical. Hint: This chapter contains some excellent verses!

_____

_____

_____

_____

_____

_____

TOM'S COMMENT

I recommend Robert and Elizabeth do the following:

- Pray regularly, asking God for His wisdom (James 1:5) and His specific direction (Psalm 25:12) to deal with worldly attitudes and to manage the money God entrusts to them (1 Corinthians 4:2). In Psalm 32:8, God promised, "I will instruct you and teach you in the way you should go; I will counsel you with my loving eye on you."

- Ask God to enable them to be content with His provision. In Luke 3:14, John the Baptist said, "Be content with your pay."

- Meditate daily on God's word (Joshua 1:8) to transform the way they think (Romans 12:1–2) to how God thinks.

First Corinthians 2:16 says we should "have the mind of Christ," and 2 Corinthians 10:5 says, "We take captive every thought to make it obedient to Christ."

- Commit to serving God, not money. Joshua said, "As for me and my household, we will serve the LORD" (Joshua 24:15).

- Develop and implement a budget. In Luke 14:28–30, Christ admonished us to plan ahead. Developing and following a budget is a practical way to plan your finances.

- Focus on things of eternal value, not on things of temporal value that do not last. In Colossians 3:1–2, Paul says, "Since, then, you have been raised with Christ, set your hearts on things above, where Christ is, seated at the right hand of God. Set your minds on things above, not on earthly things."

- Make giving to God's work a priority, as giving helps one overcome selfishness and greed. Proverbs 3:9–10 says, "Honor the LORD with your wealth, with the firstfruits of all your crops; then your barns will be filled to overflowing, and your vats will brim over with new wine." In other words, *giving generously to God's work with the right heart attitude is an antidote to selfishness and greed.*

- Thank God regularly for His provision. Psalm 118:1 says, "Give thanks to the LORD, for he is good; his love endures forever."

2. Scripture Application #1

Please read the following verse and consider its relevance to Robert and Elizabeth's situation. Does this Scripture apply to them in any way? Write your thoughts before you look at Tom's comments.

> "You shall not covet your neighbor's house. You shall not covet your neighbor's wife, or his male or female servant, his ox or donkey, or anything that belongs to your neighbor" (Exodus 20:17).

_____

_____

_____

TOM'S COMMENT

Robert and Elizabeth covet what others have, buy things they cannot afford, and accumulate significant debt. Now they are suffering the consequences. They must repent of a covetous heart and follow God's commandment to not covet what others have.

Further, they need to meditate on key Scriptures like Joshua 1:8, Philippians 4:11–13, Hebrews 13:5, and Luke 3:14. In this way, they can allow God, through His word and by His Spirit, to change the way they think about and manage money (Romans 12:2).

3. Case Study #2: A Single Woman with a Godly Money Mindset

Rebekah is a single woman who earns an average income, spends wisely, and stays within her budget. She also prioritizes giving the first 10 per cent of her income to God's work. Although she lives modestly, she is satisfied with God's provision and her standard of living.

She is not concerned that many of her friends have larger homes, more expensive automobiles, and designer clothing. Actually, *she rarely thinks about it.* Instead, she devotes her time and energy to regular church involvement and ministering to several family members.

Although Rebekah is competent in her current job, she refuses several promotions because the new position requires considerable overtime. Above all else, she desires to maintain a balanced lifestyle, which enables her to invest sufficient time in ministry and daily quality time with the Lord. Her greatest joy comes from her time in prayer, quiet reflection, and ministering to others.

Whenever Rebekah has a financial need beyond her means, she prayerfully asks God to provide instead of seeking other sources of income, like borrowing money—then waits patiently on the Lord for His provision.

As a result, her faith continues to grow as God responds to her prayers and meets her specific needs in unusual ways. This spurs Rebekah on to even greater faith as she delights in seeing God's mighty hand at work. In response, she cultivates a life of praise, worship, and gratitude for her many blessings.

QUESTION #1

How does Rebekah demonstrate godly attitudes in her way of thinking? Please list them, and provide a Scripture reference for each example of a godly attitude where possible. If necessary, review the preceding Scripture verses, then write your answers before looking at Tom's comments and suggested solutions.

_____

_____

_____

_____

_____

_____

TOM'S COMMENT

Rebekah demonstrates the following godly attitudes.

- Rebekah is content with God's provision (1 Timothy 6:6–8).

- She puts God first and trusts Him to meet her needs (Matthew 6:31–33).

- Her joy comes from a close relationship with Jesus Christ (John 10:27; Galatians 5:22–23).

- She has a thankful heart, particularly for God's provision (Psalm 118:1).

- She faithfully and cheerfully gives to God's work (2 Corinthians 9:6–7).

- She loves the Lord wholeheartedly, not money or material things (Matthew 22:37–38).

- She has a thankful attitude for the way God cares and provides for her every need (Psalm 107:8–9).

- She treasures things of eternal value, not temporal things (Colossians 3:1–2).

159

- She makes it a priority to serve God (Joshua 24:24).

- She trusts God completely (Proverbs 3:5–6).

QUESTION #2

Aside from her godly attitudes, what actions does Rebekah display that are consistent with God's word? Please list them, and provide a Scripture where applicable.

_____

_____

_____

_____

_____

_____

TOM'S COMMENT

The following outline Rebekah's actions that are in line with God's word.

- She faithfully gives the first 10 per cent of her income to God's work (Proverbs 3:9–10).

- She develops and implements a budget (Luke 14:28–30) to ensure she lives within the income God provides for her.

- She spends quality time with the Lord daily, praying and reading the Bible (Mark 1:35).

- She declines work promotions to maintain a balanced lifestyle and the ability to minister to others as God directs (John 6:38).

QUESTION #3

In light of God's word, are Rebekah's priorities in her life correct? Please explain with a Scripture reference where able.

_____

_____

_____

TOM'S COMMENT

Yes, absolutely! Rebekah's attitudes concerning money and material things are right and godly as she focuses on things of eternal value (Colossians 3:1–2). For example, she prioritizes her relationship with God and lives the way God desires her to live according to His word.

She clearly has a close relationship with the Lord (John 10:27), as she enjoys God's peace (John 14:27) and His joy (1 Peter 1:8), and she faithfully serves Him in ministry, in her family relationships, and likely in her workplace. In John 16:33, Jesus said, "I have told you these things, so that in me _you may have peace_" (emphasis added).

QUESTION #4

Should Rebekah accept a work promotion? Why or why not?

_____

_____

_____

TOM'S COMMENT

Rebekah rightly turns down work promotions because she recognizes that overtime hours would result in an _unbalanced_ *lifestyle*. Consequently, she would have less time for things of eternal value, like church participation and ministry to family members. But, most importantly, she would have less time to pray and study God's word, which is essential for spiritual growth and development.

QUESTION #5

Would it be wrong for another Christian to accept such a promotion? Please explain your answer, and provide a Scripture reference where able.

_____

_____

_____

_____

_____

_____

TOM'S COMMENT

Depending on one's specific circumstances, it may not be wrong for another Christian to accept a work promotion. The important thing is that every Christian must spend quality time with the Lord, praying and listening to God's voice (1 Kings 19:11–12) to determine God's will concerning any significant decisions, including career advancements.

While some Christians could accept such a promotion and still maintain a balanced lifestyle, others may not. Either way, there is no substitute for an intimate relationship with Jesus Christ to ensure you are doing what God wants you to do (Luke 22:42). In John 10:2–4, Jesus said:

"The one who enters by the gate is the shepherd of the sheep. The gatekeeper opens the gate for him, and the sheep listen to his voice. He calls his own sheep by name and leads them out. When he has brought out all his own, he goes on ahead of them, and his sheep follow him because they know his voice."

4. How Well Do You Recognize God's Voice?

Please think about this: How well do you recognize *God's voice* when He speaks to you in His word, by His Spirit, or through biblical counsel?

_____

_____

_____

_____

_____

_____

TOM'S COMMENT

Over the years, I have developed a close personal relationship with the Lord by meditating on various Scriptures, reading quality Christian books, and praying regularly. As a result, I am usually able to discern what the Lord wants me to do. My relationship with the Lord is still imperfect because I am imperfect, but I continue to grow and develop it!

Because of God's mercy and grace, He is extremely patient with me even when I fail to spend quality time in prayer or quietly listen for His voice. In John 10:27, Jesus said, "My sheep listen to my voice; I know them, and they follow me." Further, Psalm

85:8 says, "I will listen to what God the LORD says; he promises peace to his people, his faithful servants."

Most often, God speaks to me through His word (Psalm 119:105) and, to a lesser extent, to my heart by the Holy Spirit that lives within me. Before making any significant financial decisions, I always spend time in prayer to ask the Lord to give me His peace if He wants me to move forward with a particular decision if that is His will. On the other hand, if He does not want me to go ahead, I ask Him to give me a lack of peace, usually by feeling uneasy or apprehensive about a decision.

I committed my life to the Lord Jesus Christ on April 12, 1981, and I can confidently say that God is faithful to guide and direct His children every step of the way. Psalm 25:12 says, "Who, then, are those who fear the LORD? He will instruct them in the ways they should choose." The Lord desires to give you His wisdom (James 1:5), if you would devote the time and effort to develop an intimate relationship with Him.

To learn more about discerning God's specific will for your life, please watch our eight-part 28-minute television show, "Discerning God's Will in Managing Money," on our website at www.coplandfinancialministries.org.

5. Scripture Application #2

Are the following Scripture verses relevant to Rebekah's situation? Think about this, and write your comments for each verse.

"Godliness with contentment is great gain. For we brought nothing into the world, and we can take nothing out of it.

But if we have food and clothing, we will be content with that" (1 Timothy 6:6–8).

_____

_____

_____

_____

_____

TOM'S COMMENT

Rebekah is a godly woman who is content with God's provision. Scripture is clear that this is God's desire and will result in "great gain."

> "Since, then, you have been raised with Christ, set your hearts on things above, where Christ is, seated at the right hand of God. Set your minds on things above, not on earthly things" (Colossians 3:1–2).

_____

_____

_____

_____

_____

TOM'S COMMENT

Rebekah's heart focuses on "things above"—things of eternal value, such as her relationship with God, and she lives the life God wants for her. Therefore, since her heart is focused on things of eternal value, it makes sense that she has a godly attitude toward money and material things.

"Peace I leave with you; my peace I give you. I do not give to you as the world gives. Do not let your hearts be troubled and do not be afraid" (John 14:27).

_____

_____

_____

TOM'S COMMENT

Since Rebekah looks to God and not money for peace, joy, and happiness, it should be no surprise that she experiences just that.

"My God will meet all your needs according to the riches of his glory in Christ Jesus" (Philippians 4:19).

_____

_____

_____

TOM'S COMMENT

Rebekah trusts the Lord to meet her needs; she does not trust her own ability to provide for herself or rely on creditors like a bank.

"Let them give thanks to the LORD for his unfailing love and his wonderful deeds for mankind, for he satisfies the thirsty and fills the hungry with good things" (Psalm 107:8–9).

_____

_____

_____

TOM'S COMMENT

Rebekah thanks God regularly for His provision, and He clearly blesses her and meets all of her needs.

6. Case Study #3: A Couple Are Blessed with Business Success

Enzo and Sofia started a business many years ago. Initially, things were challenging because their cash flow was tight and profits were low. Even so, they put God first in every way they could, such as giving 10 per cent of their income to the Lord's work, being honest in their business dealings, paying off debt, and putting people before profits.

Further, the couple prayed daily for God to give them wisdom and direction in managing their business. In turn, the Lord blessed their business with significant growth in response to their obedience and prayers.

Several years later, Enzo and Sofia felt led by the Lord *to limit their personal lifestyle, even as their income increased.* Therefore, they asked God to direct them regarding specific lifestyle changes.

As time passed, God prospered their business beyond their imagination, enabling them to give even more to God's work. It was an incredible joy to be able to give so generously, and they continued to thank God for His provision. Today, Enzo and Sofia contribute approximately 70 per cent of their income to God's work every year, amounting to hundreds of thousands of dollars!

Despite their wealth, most of their friends and relatives are unaware of their financial status or generous giving. Enzo and

Sofia see themselves as average Christians whom God has blessed incredibly. In their daily quiet time with the Lord, they acknowledge that their blessings are not something they deserve but simply God's gift to them.

QUESTION #1

What godly attitudes do Enzo and Sofia demonstrate? List them, and provide a Scripture reference for each godly attitude. Hint: If you can't think of any, review the ones in the preceding chart.

_____

_____

_____

_____

_____

_____

TOM'S COMMENT

Enzo and Sofia demonstrate the following godly attitudes and mindsets concerning their finances.

- They trust God to provide for their needs (Proverbs 3:5–6). For example, they show great faith in God by giving 10 per cent of their increase to God's work, *even when their income was low* (Proverbs 3:9–10).

- They are honest in all of their business dealings (Deuteronomy 25:15–16).

- They are humble and do not flaunt their financial success. Others are unaware of their high income or generosity (James 4:10).

- They are exceptionally generous in giving to the Lord's work (2 Corinthians 9:6–11).

- They regularly thank God for His provision (Psalm 107:8–9).

- Considering their commitment to putting God first, generous giving, attitude of contentment, and daily quiet times spent in prayer, it is clear that Enzo and Sofia genuinely love the Lord with all their hearts (Matthew 22:37–38).

- They faithfully serve God, not money (Matthew 6:24).

- They depend entirely upon God to provide for their every need and did so, especially during their business start-up. They continue to rely on God as they prosper (John 15:5).

- They focus on things of eternal value, like giving to God's work rather than spending the extra money on themselves. As a result, they are building up treasures in heaven (Matthew 6:19–21).

QUESTION #2

In addition to their godly attitudes, what *actions* do Enzo and Sofia take that are consistent with God's word? Please list them and provide a relevant Scripture reference where able.

_____

_____

_____

_____

_____

_____

TOM'S COMMENT

Enzo and Sofia pray daily for God's wisdom (James 1:5) and direction (Psalm 32:8). Further, they display the following actions.

- They give to God's work by faithfully tithing (Malachi 3:8–10; Leviticus 27:30–32), as they did even when their income was modest.

- They put God first in everything (Matthew 6:31–33) and depend upon the Lord (John 15:1–8) for His provision.

- They put people ahead of profits, demonstrating their love for God (Mark 12:30).

QUESTION #3

When Enzo and Sofia's business struggled during the start-up phase, was it important they intentionally give 10 per cent of their income to God's work? If so, why?

_____

_____

_____

_____

_____

_____

TOM'S COMMENT

Yes, it was vital for them to prioritize giving to God's work even with a modest income because it showed the condition of their hearts. Further, Jesus said, "The one who is faithful in a very little thing is also faithful in much; and the one who is unrighteous in a very little thing is also unrighteous in much" (Luke 16:10 NASB).

According to the parable of the talents (Matthew 25:14–30), the "master", who is God, entrusted more to the faithful servants. The bottom line is that if you don't put God first when you have a modest income, why would you put God first when your income is higher?

Over the last four decades, I have seen many cases where a person who is not faithful to the Lord when their income is modest; is not faithful to the Lord when their income is much higher. The reason is that they continue to apply the same worldly attitudes about money management, even when they have a lot of money. Ultimately, *it is about priorities and one's heart attitude toward money and material things, not the amount of income one has!*

QUESTION #4

Do you think Enzo and Sofia enjoy a close relationship with God? If yes, please identify their attitudes and actions that reflect this. Has their intimacy with the Lord helped them avoid worldly attitudes toward money?

_____

_____

_____

_____

_____

_____

TOM'S COMMENT

Yes, definitely. Enzo and Sofia's attitudes and actions reflect a strong personal relationship with the Lord. Here are some examples.

- They spend quality time daily with the Lord in prayer (James 5:16).

- They read His word regularly (2 Timothy 3:16–17).

- They "seek first the kingdom of God" (Matthew 6:33) and give God first place in their lives in every area (Joshua 24:24).

- In light of their generous giving and modest lifestyle, they clearly *focus on things of eternal value* (Colossians 3:1–2), not on things that are temporary, like accumulating money and material things (Matthew 6:19–21).

- They praise God for their many blessings. Psalm 145:3 says, "Great is the LORD and most worthy of praise; his greatness no one can fathom."

- Notwithstanding their high income, they are humble (1 Peter 5:5).

- Through their close relationship with God, they learn God's truth, which teaches them to avoid worldly attitudes related to money and material things. Psalm 25:5 says, "Guide me in your truth and teach me, for you are God my Savior, and my hope is in you all day long."

7. Scripture Application #3

Discuss the relevance and application of the following verses in relation to Enzo and Sofia's situation. Then write your comments for each verse before looking at Tom's comments.

"You may say to yourself, "My power and the strength of my hands have produced this wealth for me." But remember the Lᴏʀᴅ your God, for it is he who gives you the ability to produce wealth" (Deuteronomy 8:17–18).

TOM'S COMMENT

Enzo and Sofia consider themselves average Christians whom God has blessed. Hence, they acknowledge that God blesses them with a successful business and the ability to manage it. As a result, they are humble and praise God for His wonderful provision.

But, unfortunately, most successful people develop big egos, and what does God say about this? In James 4:6, we are reminded that "God opposes the proud but shows favor to the humble." Further, Enzo and Sofia follow God's admonition in James 4:10, which says, "Humble yourselves before the Lord, and he will lift you up."

"Remember this: Whoever sows sparingly will also reap sparingly, and whoever sows generously will also reap generously. Each of you should give what you have decided in your heart to give, not reluctantly or under compulsion, for God loves a cheerful giver …

Now he who supplies seed to the sower and bread for food will also supply and increase your store of seed and will enlarge the harvest of your righteousness. You will be enriched in every way so that you can be generous on every occasion, and through us your generosity will result in thanksgiving to God" (2 Corinthians 9:6–7, 10–11).

_____

_____

_____

_____

_____

TOM'S COMMENT

Enzo and Sofia give quite generously to God's work, which results in God blessing them with more income, so that they can be even more generous. In addition, fixing their lifestyle is an important decision that significantly impacts their ability to give at a much higher level.

Unfortunately, most people raise their standard of living when their income increases and spend more money on themselves. As Christians, when God entrusts us with more money, we should *raise our standard of giving rather than raise our standard of living!*

Jesus said, "I am the vine; you are the branches. If you remain in me and I in you, you will bear much fruit; apart from me you can do nothing" (John 15:5).

_____

_____

_____

_____

_____

TOM'S COMMENT

Enzo and Sofia maintain an intimate relationship with Jesus Christ, which, from a biblical perspective, is the primary reason they manage money well and give so generously.

According to Jesus's teaching in John 15:2, "He [the Father] cuts off every branch in me that bears no fruit, while every branch that does bear fruit he prunes so that it will be even more fruitful." Indeed, Enzo and Sofia bear even more fruit because of their close and abiding relationship with the Lord.

> "Do not store up for yourselves treasures on earth, where moth and rust destroy, and where thieves break in and steal. But store up for yourselves treasures in heaven, where neither moth nor rust destroys, and where thieves do not break in or steal; for where your treasure is, there your heart will be also" (Matthew 6:19–21 NASB).

_____

_____

_____

TOM'S COMMENT

As Enzo and Sofia manage the money God entrusts to them according to biblical principles, they build up for themselves "treasures in heaven." Additionally, their generosity to God's work will result in eternal *spiritual benefits and rewards* (through the ministries they support) when they enter into glory with the Lord Jesus Christ.

Mark 9:41 (NLT) assures, "If anyone gives you even a cup of water because you belong to the Messiah, I tell you the truth, that person will surely be rewarded."

Further, in Matthew 16:27, Jesus said, "The Son of Man is going to come in his Father's glory with his angels, and then he will reward each person according to what they have done."

F. PRACTICAL APPLICATION OF PRINCIPLES RELATED TO GODLY VERSUS UNGODLY ATTITUDES TOWARD MONEY

Please review the preceding comparison between godly and worldly attitudes concerning money management. Then prayerfully ask the Lord to reveal (a) your godly attitudes toward money and (b) the ungodly attitudes you struggle with concerning money.

Then please list them under the following two categories:

GODLY ATTITUDES	WORLDLY ATTITUDES

TOM'S COMMENT

This section involves personal responses that may vary from person to person. I highly recommend that every reader of this book review the preceding Scriptures, meditate upon them, and allow them to transform the way you think about and manage money.

Be encouraged that we all struggle with some worldly attitudes pertaining to our finances—yet, we often don't see it. If you are married, pray about this with your spouse, sharing honestly with each other. If you are single, ask the Lord to connect you with a godly and trustworthy accountability partner.

1. Personal Exercise #1

1. Take time to pray, asking the Lord to enable you to maintain the godly attitudes you identified. If God speaks to your heart, write your thoughts here.

_____

_____

_____

_____

_____

_____

_____

_____

_____

2. As discussed, some Christians struggle with ungodly, worldly attitudes toward money. Please pray and ask God, by the power of the Holy Spirit, to enable you to overcome any worldly attitudes you identified. Then write your thoughts here.

_____

_____

_____

_____

_____

_____

_____

_____

_____

3. As a practical matter, work on one worldly attitude at a time by identifying the one you believe the Lord wants you to work on first—likely the one that most contributed to your financial difficulty. Then, for the next thirty days, meditate on a relevant Scripture verse that deals specifically with this ungodly attitude.

I encourage you to commit this verse to memory to allow the *living word of God* to penetrate your heart, renew your mind, and transform how you think about and manage money and material things (Romans 12:2). *If you are eager to learn and grow, work on multiple verses at a time!*

2. Scripture Meditation

Review and meditate upon the following verses and explain their practical application to changing worldly attitudes into godly attitudes.

After you've read each one, write them out to help you remember these important biblical principles.

"I urge you, brothers and sisters, in view of God's mercy, to offer your bodies as a living sacrifice, holy and pleasing to God—this is your true and proper worship. Do not conform to the pattern of this world, but be transformed by the renewing of your mind. Then you will be able to test and approve what God's will is—his good, pleasing and perfect will" (Romans 12:1–2).

_____

_____

_____

_____

_____

_____

TOM'S COMMENT

What we do is determined by how we think. Unfortunately, many Christians make worldly decisions regarding finances because they think in ungodly or worldly ways. Therefore, it is critical for followers of Jesus Christ to be transformed by the renewing of their minds—to change their mindsets and faulty thinking patterns. Once they learn to think wisely about money and material things, godly actions will naturally flow from those with the "mind of Christ" (1 Corinthians 2:16).

"Keep this Book of the Law always on your lips; meditate on it day and night, so that you may be careful to do everything written in it. Then you will be prosperous and successful" (Joshua 1:8).

_____

_____

_____

TOM'S COMMENT

God instructs us to meditate on His word "day and night" (to be immersed in it) to ensure we learn to think God's way, act God's way, and conform to His will for us. Learning to think God's way leads to godly attitudes and biblically-based stewardship of money and material things.

"These commandments that I give you today are to be on your hearts. Impress them on your children. Talk about them when you sit at home and when you walk along the road, when you lie down and when you get up. Tie them as symbols on your hands and bind them on your foreheads. Write them on the doorframes of your houses and on your gates" (Deuteronomy 6:6–9).

_____

_____

_____

TOM'S COMMENT

Unfortunately, we cannot automatically erase our worldly mindsets. Still, we can *fill our minds with God's word* by prayerfully reading and memorizing Scripture verses that apply to our situation. In so doing, the discipline of daily meditation on

God's word will help us adopt God's way of thinking. In turn, we are more likely to make decisions consistent with His will and plan for our lives, financial or otherwise.

3. Personal Exercise #2

1. Write the above Scriptures in the space provided to help you remember these important biblical financial principles.

_____

_____

_____

_____

_____

_____

_____

_____

2. Please consider other ways to replace worldly attitudes toward money and material things with godly attitudes. Then list them here before reading Tom's comment. To help, note Tom's following nine suggestions.

_____

_____

_____

_____

_____

_____

_____

_____

TOM'S COMMENT

In the following section are other ideas to help replace worldly attitudes with godly attitudes concerning money and material things.

4. TOM'S NINE SUGGESTIONS TO REPLACE WORLDLY ATTITUDES TOWARD MONEY AND MATERIAL THINGS WITH GODLY ATTITUDES

1. Attend a small-group Bible study related to finances. I strongly recommend our 12-week series based on my book, "Financial Management God's Way." We have seen the most significant and permanent changes in how people manage their money from participating in this program. Alternatively, you can watch the online interactive version on our website or join a small group—most are held as a virtual Zoom meeting, so it doesn't matter where you live. For further details, check our website at www.coplandfinancialministries.org.

2. Develop and maintain a genuine personal relationship with Jesus Christ, who said, "Apart from me, you can do nothing" (see John 15:1–8).

3. Work regularly with an accountability partner who understands God's word on finances. Ideally, your accountability partner should be your spouse if you are married.

4. Pray regularly and ask the Lord to enable you to be content with His provision (Philippians 4:11–13), to

develop an attitude of contentment, and to learn to think God's way.

5. Focus on things of eternal value, such as the salvation of souls, Christian ministry, and giving generously of your time and resources to God's work. Cherish these things because, as Jesus said in Matthew 6:21, "Where your treasure is, there your heart will be also."

6. Confess any financial-related sin (1 John 1:9), which means you agree with God that you have sinned and are ready to repent and turn from violating biblical financial principles to managing money God's way, which you can accomplish with His help. Please note the list of "financial-related sins" in the previous comparison chart.

7. Limit your exposure to the media—especially those that stir up ungodly desires, like advertisements that encourage extraneous spending (2 Corinthians 10:3–5; John 17:15–16).

8. Every day, ask the Lord to help you develop godly attitudes and thinking concerning money and material things, so that you may develop "the mind of Christ" (1 Corinthians 2:16).

9. Please go to www.coplandfinancialministries.org and watch the three 30-minute shows, "Developing Godly Attitudes Toward Money," which are a part of the "Handling Money God's Way" series. Be sure also to view the three 30-minute shows on the topic of a "Secular Versus Biblical Perspective on Money."

5. Summary of Godly Versus Ungodly Attitudes Toward Money

Unfortunately, many people, including Christians, have worldly attitudes or mindsets when it comes to managing money and material things. In my experience, it is often due to a lack of understanding of what the Bible says about finances, or it could be a worldly attitude with respect to money and material things. As well, most people are short-sighted and need to *think more deeply about eternity*. As such, they focus on the temporal, like money and material things.

This is a sad reality, since God's word could not be clearer that every Christian will be judged for what they did with the time, talents, and money God entrusted them. Specifically, 2 Corinthians 5:10 says, "We must all appear before the judgment seat of Christ, so that each of us may receive what is due us for the things done while in the body, whether good or bad."

Every Christian will face a special judgment called the "Judgment [Bema] Seat of Christ", *based on what they did with the resources God entrusted to them* while here on earth. First Corinthians 4:2 says, "Now it is required that those who have been given a trust must prove faithful." In other words, faithfulness to God entails managing money according to God's specific will and financial principles as outlined in His word! Therefore, believers who have been faithful in managing money God's way will receive many rewards in heaven (Matthew 16:27), while those who have not been faithful will have few rewards.

For clarity, all Christians who have accepted Jesus Christ as their personal Saviour and Lord will have their names written in the Lamb's Book of Life (Revelation 21:27), will be forgiven of their sins and will spend eternity in heaven. However, it is unfortunate that some Christians will have very few eternal rewards because of their worldly attitudes and selfish spending, rather than investing in God's kingdom.

Having said that, you must provide for the needs of your own family (1 Timothy 5:8), but not necessarily their wants and desires (Matthew 6:31–33). Unfortunately, many Christians spend too much money on selfish desires and build up treasures on earth instead of treasures in heaven (Matthew 6:19–21).

Remember, in 1 Timothy 6:7, the apostle Paul says, "We brought nothing into the world, and we can take nothing out of it." So it is essential to always remember that money is temporary, and we are responsible for managing it God's way for a relatively short time while we are on earth, which is brief compared to eternity!

However, suppose you adopt godly attitudes toward money and material things and use them for eternal purposes, such as evangelism, discipleship, and giving generously to God's work. Then, when you get to heaven, you will hear the words from our Lord Jesus Christ that you long to hear: "Well done, good and faithful servant! You have been faithful with a few things; I will put you in charge of many things. Come and share your master's happiness!" (Matthew 25:21).

And what could be better than that!?

V.

STORE UP TREASURES IN HEAVEN, NOT ON EARTH

A. KEY BIBLICAL PRINCIPLE

How we manage the money, material things, time, and talents that God has entrusted us while we are on the earth will result in rewards or lack of rewards when we get to heaven.

1. Store Up Treasures in Heaven

In the Sermon on the Mount teaching in Matthew 6:19–21, Jesus said:

> "Do not store up for yourselves treasures on earth, where moths and vermin destroy, and where thieves break in and steal. But store up for yourselves treasures in heaven, where moths and vermin do not destroy, and where thieves do not break in and steal. For where your treasure is, there your heart will be also."

Allow Christ's words to penetrate your heart as He reveals how one's eternal perspective determines their earthly priorities. The Lord's instructions are clear: During our lifetime, we must focus on storing up treasures in heaven that will last forever rather than earthly treasures that do not last.

B. QUESTIONS TO CONTEMPLATE AND TOM'S COMMENTS

QUESTION #1

What are treasures in heaven? Think about this for a moment before writing your response.

_____

_____

_____

_____

_____

_____

_____

_____

_____

_____

_____

_____

TOM'S COMMENT

From a biblical perspective, "treasures in heaven" refers to those things of eternal value that we will treasure when we reach heaven. Such things include but are not limited to the salvation of people, our relationship with Jesus Christ, and the rewards (Matthew 25:14–30) and levels of authority (Luke 19:11–27) that God will grant us when we reach heaven.

But of course, these benefits will depend on how we manage the money, material things, and the time and talents God entrusted us while we were on earth. Please allow me to explain the rewards and the levels of authority in heaven.

1. Rewards in Heaven

In Matthew 25:14–30, in the parable of the bags of gold (also called the parable of the talents), Jesus tells of a master (who is God) who entrusted five bags of gold to one servant, two to another, and one to a third servant. After a long time (perhaps a lifetime), God returned and held the servants accountable for 100 per cent of what was entrusted to them! God said to the first two servants who invested their gold wisely, "Well done, good and faithful servant! You have been faithful with a few things; I will put you in charge of many things. Come and share your master's happiness!" As for the third servant, who was wicked and lazy and did not invest, God took away his bag of gold and gave it to the first servant, who was faithful to the Lord.

The parable of the bags of gold clearly illustrates that one day we will all be held accountable to God for 100 per cent of what He entrusted to us. However, it is uncertain when the day of accountability will come, as it could occur when Jesus returns or after we depart from this life and stand before the Lord at the "judgment seat of Christ" (2 Corinthians 5:10)—to be discussed in more detail later in this chapter and in chapter VII.

In this parable, it's interesting to note that the servant who acquired two bags of gold received the same reward as the servant who gained five bags of gold. Since we know that God gives different amounts of income to different people, don't be fooled into thinking that you are not accountable to God if you have less money than others. As Paul said in Romans 14:12, "Each of us will give an account of ourselves to God." In other words, we will all be held accountable for how we used the money He entrusted us, regardless of how much money we had.

Some of the eternal rewards of building up treasures in heaven, as promised by God to His faithful servants, are available here on earth before we enter glory, such as experiencing God's peace (John 14:27) and God's joy (Psalm 16:11).

2. Authority in Heaven

Luke 19:11–26 describes the parable of the ten minas, where a certain nobleman (who represents God) entrusted ten minas to each of his ten servants, instructing them to "Put this money to work until I come back." In time, God returned and held them accountable.

The first servant came and said, "Sir, your mina has earned ten more," to which his master replied, "Well done, my good servant! Because you have been trustworthy in a very small matter, take charge of ten cities." Then the second servant came and said, "Sir, your mina has earned five more," to which his master answered, "You take charge of five cities." And for the servant who *made no effort* to invest his master's money, even what he did have was taken from him, and he received no heavenly rewards or heavenly authority.

Considering the above parable, can you appreciate how this biblical account parallels a Christian who makes no significant effort to utilize the money, material things, time, and talents God entrusts them with for eternal purposes?

QUESTION #2

What are treasures on earth? Ponder this question before looking at Tom's comment.

_____

_____

_____

_____

_____

_____

TOM'S COMMENT

"Treasures on earth" refers to perishable things that have no lasting value, such as our money, material possessions, jobs, status or position, and various pleasures in life. But according to Jesus, our worldly investments are temporary, so we should focus on the values and priorities that align with God's values and priorities—things that build His kingdom and will last forever.

It's important to understand that what one treasures in their heart is usually reflected by what they focus on and where they spend their time, money, and energy. Note the words of Jesus in Matthew 6:21: "Where your treasure is, there your heart will be also."

In other words, if one's true treasures are in earthly things, one's heart and attention will be devoted to worldly matters. Despite what we may say, *our bank accounts and daytimers often reflect our true values and priorities!*

191

QUESTION #3

How can you follow Jesus's warning in Matthew 6:19–21 to "store up for yourselves treasures in heaven"?

_____

_____

_____

TOM'S COMMENT

Here are some important ways to "store up for yourselves treasures in heaven," which have eternal value.

1. Study and meditate on God's word concerning finances so that God can change how you think about and manage money and material things. Romans 12:2 states, "Do not conform to the pattern of this world, but be transformed by the renewing of your mind." And how do we renew our minds? The answer is in Joshua 1:8: "Keep this Book of the Law always on your lips; meditate on it day and night, so that you may be careful to do everything written in it. Then you will be prosperous and successful."

2. You should pray often and daily, asking God for His wisdom (James 1:5) and His specific direction (Psalm 32:8) to utilize the resources God has entrusted to you according to His specific will for His glory and honor.

3. Pay careful attention to what God says to you through His Word (Psalm 119:105) and His Holy Spirit (John 10:27). Once you discern what God wants you to do, obey His leading and follow through (James 1:22).

4. Invest your time, money, and resources into God's kingdom work. As the apostle Paul said in 2 Corinthians 9:6–7, "Whoever sows sparingly will also reap sparingly, and whoever sows generously will also reap generously. Each of you should give what you have decided in your heart to give, not reluctantly or under compulsion, for God loves a cheerful giver."

5. As you invest your money, time, and talents into God's work, your heart will follow! In Matthew 6:21, Jesus said, "For where your treasure is, there your heart will be also."

6. Ask the Lord to reveal where He wants you to engage in evangelism and discipleship. If the Lord can use you to influence just one person to come to know Jesus as their personal Saviour, in a million years, when you are in heaven, that person will also be in heaven. An individual's salvation is of eternal significance and utmost importance to God, so it should also be to us.

7. Be an effective witness for the Lord by managing the money He has entrusted you according to His biblical financial principles and specific will. This includes paying your creditors on time (Romans 13:8), so you can "let your light shine before others, that they may see your good deeds and glorify your Father in heaven" (Matthew 5:16).

3. It Is *Not* Selfish to "Store up Treasures in Heaven" for Yourself!

Some people believe that storing up treasures in heaven for themselves is selfish. This is *not* true. Giving to the Lord's work

193

glorifies God (2 Corinthians 9:10–11) and reveals a generous heart concerning money and material things (Philippians 2:3–4).

In simple terms, selfishness means doing things for your benefit while you are on earth, sometimes at the expense of others. Since the Lord has an infinite supply of resources, He can provide unlimited blessings on earth and in heaven to those who manage their finances and resources in a trustworthy manner.

4. A Word of Caution About "the Love of Money"

Recall from a previous chapter that "the love of money" is a root of all kinds of evil, not money in and of itself. Money is a neutral commodity—neither moral nor immoral, spiritual nor unspiritual. It's merely a tool and resource to manage while on earth. The apostle Paul warns us in 1 Timothy 6:9–10:

> "Those who want to get rich fall into temptation and a trap and into many foolish and harmful desires that plunge people into ruin and destruction. For *the love of money is a root* of all kinds of evil. Some people, eager for money, have wandered from the faith and pierced themselves with many griefs" (emphasis added).

Unfortunately, even Christians can struggle with the love of money. In the following verse (1 Timothy 6:11), Paul advises, "You, man of God, flee from all this, and pursue righteousness, godliness, faith, love, endurance and gentleness." Pursuing godly characteristics such as faith, love, righteousness, long-suffering, and gentleness results in eternal rewards.

In Ecclesiastes 5:10–11, King Solomon, once considered the wisest of all men, warned, "Whoever loves money never has enough; whoever loves wealth is never satisfied with their income … As goods increase, so do those who consume them. And what benefit are they to the owners?" And in Ecclesiastes 5:12–14, Solomon says, "As for the rich, their abundance permits them no sleep. I have seen a grievous evil under the sun: wealth hoarded to the harm of its owners, or wealth lost through some misfortune." Even in Solomon's time, money and material things never satisfied!

Sadly, from over four decades of experience as an accountant and financial adviser, I can confirm that when people have more money, they often use it for personal benefit instead of generously giving to God's work.

As highlighted by King Solomon, the biblical truth is that money and material things in themselves will never satisfy. Therefore, take time to prayerfully ask the Lord to show you the true condition of your heart concerning money (Psalm 139:23–24), and ask God to enable you to avoid being trapped by the love of money.

5. Make Sure You Serve God, Not Money!

In Matthew 6:24, Jesus said, "No one can serve two masters. Either you will hate the one and love the other, or you will be devoted to the one and despise the other. You cannot serve both God and money."

It's interesting to note that when Jesus warned that we could serve another master, that master was not self or someone else. It was money. That's because money and material things can quickly become our master.

For example, I've seen too often how money distracts even well-intentioned people from things of eternal value, such as cultivating a relationship with Christ, spending quality time with their spouse and children, and being actively involved in Christian ministry. Other areas that often suffer are a lack of investment in giving their time, talents, tithes, and offerings into Christian ministries to build the kingdom of God.

I encourage you to prayerfully consider some of the following key indicators that you may be serving money rather than God:

- Working excessively (Proverbs 23:4–5).

- Spending limited or no time with God each day (John 10:27).

- Having little or no involvement in Christian ministry (Ephesians 2:10).

- Giving minimally or infrequently to God's work (Proverbs 3:9–10).

- Leading a selfish lifestyle with no desire to contribute to God's kingdom (see the parable of the rich fool in Luke 12:15–21).

Other spiritual issues that can give rise to financial problems include the following worldly attitudes:

- Covetousness (Exodus 20:17).

- A lack of contentment (Hebrews 13:5).

- Greed (Luke 12:15).

- Selfishness (James 3:16).

- Pride (James 4:6).

6. The Significance of God's Kingdom and Things of Eternal Value

Note the words of Jesus in the parables of the hidden treasure and the pearl, which appear in Matthew 13:44–46 and illustrate the immense value of the kingdom of heaven:

> "The kingdom of heaven is like treasure hidden in a field. When a man found it, he hid it again, and then in his joy went and sold all he had and bought that field.

> "Again, the kingdom of heaven is like a merchant looking for fine pearls. When he found one of great value, he went away and sold everything he had and bought it."

God tells us that the kingdom of heaven is so valuable that, if necessary, we must be willing to give up everything we have in this life to gain the kingdom of heaven, which includes the greatest treasure of all—a personal relationship with Jesus Christ. Unlike any other relationship we will ever experience, this relationship will endure into eternity in heaven!

7. Our Relationship with Christ Must Be Our Highest Priority

The apostle Paul considered a personal relationship with Jesus Christ more important than anything else. Note what he said in Philippians 3:8:

> "What is more, I consider everything a loss compared to the surpassing worth of knowing Christ Jesus my Lord, for whose sake I have lost all things. I consider them garbage, that I may gain Christ."

Remember, if you have accepted Jesus Christ as your personal Saviour and Lord, your relationship with Christ will last *forever.* Let that sink in for a moment. The literal meaning of forever is for all of eternity! So spend quality time every day reading God's word and praying earnestly to deepen your relationship with Him.

In this way, you will be better able to hear and discern His voice (John 10:27) and His specific direction and will for whatever decisions you face. Psalm 25:12 affirms that God promises to direct our paths as it says, "Who, then, are those who fear the LORD? He will instruct them in the ways they should choose."

8. The *Best* Investment Ever Is Guaranteed by God!

People often look for the best investments to build their portfolios to save for their retirement or children's education. Indeed, that is not wrong in itself, as it is a biblical concept to plan ahead, especially concerning saving and investing to meet future needs (see the parable of the tower in Luke 14:28–30).

However, most Christians are unaware that the single best investment they could ever make is guaranteed by the King of kings and the Lord of lords! Jesus provides us with a sobering description of this in Matthew 19:29, "Everyone who has left *houses ... or fields for my sake* will receive a hundred times as much and will inherit eternal life" (emphasis added).

In other words, we can give up money and material things, such as houses and land, which are temporal, and receive a hundred times as much in eternity. In fact, God guarantees a ten thousand per cent return on our investment! What an incredible promise from God! There are no financial institutions on earth that offer such a return!

Please understand I am not teaching a prosperity gospel. It is not appropriate to give money to God's work only to expect God to give you a hundredfold return. God will never bless or reward our selfish motives when we give to get. Proverbs 16:2 says "All a person's ways seem pure to them, but motives are weighed by the LORD."

God desires that we give to His work out of our sincere love for Him. In this way, we demonstrate our appreciation for everything He has provided, especially the gift of salvation and eternal life we have been given through Jesus Christ (Ephesians 2:8–9). Further, we should give to God's work and expect nothing in return (Luke 6:35–36).

Suppose a Christian manages money according to biblical principles, including developing and implementing a budget, incurring minimal debt, being content with God's provision, and giving generously to God's work (with the right heart). In that case, since they have demonstrated they are faithful with a small amount, God may very well entrust them with more (see the parable of the ten minas in Luke 19:11–27).

Alternatively, God can bless faithful Christians with good health, a wonderful marriage, a good relationship with their children, and an effective ministry for the Lord.

Another point I would make is that giving generously to God's work should be a priority, as Proverbs 3:9–10 says: "Honor the LORD with your wealth, with the firstfruits of all your crops; then your barns will be filled to overflowing, and your vats will brim over with new wine." However, providing for your family's needs is also critically important. First Timothy 5:8 says, "Anyone who does not provide for their relatives, and especially for their own household, has denied the faith and is worse than an unbeliever."

199

9. There Will Be Rewards in Heaven for Biblical Money Management and Godly Character

God promises to reward godly stewardship of all His blessings. In Matthew 16:27, Jesus said, "The Son of Man is going to come in his Father's glory with his angels, and then he will reward each person according to what they have done." Some of these rewards will come from managing money according to biblical principles and God's specific will.

God will also provide rewards in heaven for godly character. Second Peter 1:5–11 states:

"Make every effort to add to your faith goodness; and to goodness, knowledge; and to knowledge, self-control; and to self-control, perseverance; and to perseverance, godliness; and to godliness, mutual affection; and to mutual affection, love. For if you possess these qualities in increasing measure, they will keep you from being ineffective and unproductive in your knowledge of our Lord Jesus Christ. But whoever does not have them is nearsighted and blind, forgetting that they have been cleansed from their past sins.

"Therefore, my brothers and sisters, make every effort to confirm your calling and election. For if you do these things, you will never stumble, and you will receive a rich welcome into the eternal kingdom of our Lord and Savior Jesus Christ."

This passage teaches us that we will be rewarded in heaven if we possess godly characteristics while on earth. Further, one's godly character traits of self-control (including self-discipline related to spending), kindness, godliness (including giving to God's work), and our love for Christ should be the number one reason for serving Christ and giving generously to His work.

And what is the likely outcome of following these biblical principles? God's Word promises you will "receive a rich welcome into the eternal kingdom of our Lord and Savior Jesus Christ." There is nothing more promising than that!

10. Remember That Money and Material Things Are Temporary

In 1 Timothy 6:6–8, the apostle Paul said:

> "Godliness with contentment is great gain. For we brought nothing into the world, and we can take nothing out of it. But if we have food and clothing, we will be content with that."

Note Ecclesiastes 5:15:

> "Everyone comes naked from their mother's womb, and as everyone comes, so they depart. They take nothing from their toil that they can carry in their hands."

It is essential to understand that all of your earthly possessions will be lost when you die, but whatever you give with a godly motive, in the name of Christ, will come back to you a hundred times over in heaven! (Matthew 19:29).

Indeed, you cannot take your money with you. But in a sense, you can "send it on ahead" by managing your finances God's way and giving generously to God's work while on earth. In other words, you can invest the money God entrusts to you in a way that will result in eternal benefits for you and those you bless.

11. Keep Eternity in Mind

Many Christians save for retirement, which is consistent with biblical principles and the advice often given by financial advisers to think thirty years ahead (Proverbs 21:5; Luke 14:28–30). This is fine from a worldly perspective, but we should think *30 million years* ahead from a biblical and eternal perspective!

In light of this, I encourage you to ask yourself: What am I doing with the money God has entrusted to me that will impact eternity? Remember that giving to God's work and serving the Lord is "credited to your heavenly account." In Philippians 4:17, Paul said, "Not that I desire your gifts; what I desire is that more be credited to your account."

Put another way, the Lord keeps track of everything we do for Him—in particular, how we invest and use His money (Haggai 2:8). Consider that every time you give to the Lord's work, there is a credit to your "heavenly account," which will benefit you and others when you get to heaven!

In summary, investing money in God's work is an excellent way to *convert a temporal asset, such as money, into an eternal asset with eternal value.*

12. Give to the Poor as Part of Your Regular Giving

Take note of what Jesus said in Luke 12:33 about giving to the poor:

> "Sell your possessions and give to the poor. Provide purses for yourselves that will not wear out, a treasure in heaven that will never fail, where no thief comes near and no moth destroys."

Wow! When we give to the poor, Jesus affirms that God will reward us with a treasure in heaven that will never be exhausted. Therefore, as we give to God's work while on earth, the blessings and treasures in heaven will benefit others and us for all eternity!

13. When You Give, Do Not Boast about Your Giving

Note Jesus's words of caution in Matthew 6:1–4:

> "Be careful not to practice your righteousness in front of others to be seen by them. If you do, you will have no reward from your Father in heaven.

> "So when you give to the needy, do not announce it with trumpets, as the hypocrites do in the synagogues and on the streets, to be honored by others. Truly I tell you, they have received their reward in full. But when you give to the needy, do not let you left hand know what your right hand is doing, so that your giving may be in secret. Then your Father, who sees what is done in secret, will reward you."

According to this passage, those who give with the right heart attitude will be rewarded by our Father, but those who do not give with the right heart attitude will lose their reward. Therefore, be careful not to allow pride to creep into your heart when you give! You can avoid this by keeping your giving to the Lord's work confidential.

In addition, God provides rewards during our earthly lives (Matthew 25:14–30), but our greatest rewards will come in heaven and last forever!

14. A Paradigm Shift to Focus on Things of Eternal Value

Simply put, a paradigm shift is a change from the usual way of thinking about or doing something to a new way. In light of this, Christians need to "make the paradigm shift" from acquiring material things and spending money on wants and desires to investing money and resources into God's kingdom, which results in great and eternal rewards. This is why Jesus told us, "Do not store up for yourselves treasures on earth ... But store up for yourselves treasures in heaven" (Matthew 6:19–21).

Once a believer understands their stewardship responsibilities over God's money and resources and that they will receive incredible rewards in heaven for using them for eternal purposes, there should be a stark difference between the money management priorities for a Christian and a non-Christian.

Unfortunately, most Christians manage and use money similarly to nonbelievers—buying things they don't need, using credit liberally, and accumulating debt (sadly, as their debt increases, their giving inevitably decreases).

In my experience, few Christians can be trusted with a lot of money because when most receive more money, *they raise their standard of living instead of raise their standard of giving!* Likewise, some believers hoard money and material things, resulting in few or no rewards in heaven.

15. Heaven Is Our Forever Home, Not Earth

The truth is that most people store up treasures on earth because they think of earth as their home. But in reality, this world is not our home, as we are here for a relatively short period compared to the time frame of heaven, which is forever!

I encourage you to read Hebrews chapter 11, which describes "faith in action." These patriarchs, matriarchs, and great people of God lived as aliens and strangers on earth, longing for a better country—a heavenly one. They recognized that earth was not their home, but a temporary place to sojourn while living. They understood their eternal home and final destiny to be in heaven.

In Philippians 3:20, Paul said, "Our citizenship is in heaven. And we eagerly await a Savior from there, the Lord Jesus Christ." Christians must remember that our real home and citizenship are in heaven, not on earth. Therefore, investing God's money and resources into people and ministries to build His kingdom and fulfill His will on earth makes perfect sense—the long-term result and benefit is eternal rewards in heaven!

16. Be Willing to Adopt a More Moderate Lifestyle

Moses was a godly man who had his priorities right concerning money and material things. Hebrews 11:25–26 describes how Moses "chose to be mistreated along with the people of God rather than to enjoy the fleeting pleasures of sin. He regarded disgrace for the sake of Christ as of greater value than the treasures of Egypt because *he was looking ahead to his reward*" (emphasis added).

Moses understood that heaven, not earth, was his true home. Thus, he used the time, money, and resources God entrusted him to serve the Lord faithfully as he looked ahead to his eternal reward in heaven.

17. Faithfulness to God Is Critical

First Corinthians 4:2 states, "Now it is required that those who have been given a trust must prove faithful." Faithfulness to God is critical! Here are questions the Lord may ask you at the "judgment seat of Christ" (see 2 Corinthians 5:10):

1. During your time on earth, what did you do with the money, material things, time, and talents I entrusted to you? Did you spend them on your selfish desires or use them for eternal purposes?

2. Did you use these resources wisely and unselfishly to bring glory to Me according to My biblical principles?

Those who profess to have a personal relationship with Jesus Christ need to understand that how they manage the money and material things God entrusts to them on earth will determine whether or not they receive rewards in heaven.

For those who manage money God's way and give generously to His work, *there will be tremendous rewards in heaven that will last for eternity. This is because they* live with an eternal perspective and invest their money, time, giftings, and talents accordingly.

C. CASE STUDY AND TOM'S COMMENTS

1. Case Study: A Married Couple Pursue Worldly Riches

Dave and Diane are a married Christian couple who work full-time and earn above-average salaries. They attend a Bible-believing church but have limited involvement in their church or any other Christian ministry.

Dave enjoys driving expensive cars, which he exchanges every few years, resulting in hefty car payments. He also likes to golf and pays significant annual fees for belonging to a prestigious golf club.

For her part, Diane enjoys trips to the shopping mall to buy clothes, household goods, and various things, most of which are wants and desires as opposed to necessities.

Because of their undisciplined spending habits, Dave and Diane spend all their regular income and have no savings. Not surprisingly, they are forced to use credit when an unforeseen expenditure arises, increasing their debt load. Their substantial monthly expenses and ongoing debt accumulation only allow them to give 2 per cent of their income to God's work, which is very little.

QUESTION #1

Are Dave and Diane storing up treasures in heaven, or is their focus on treasures on earth? Explain your answer before looking at Tom's comment.

_____

_____

_____

TOM'S COMMENT

Dave and Diane focus on storing up treasures on earth "where moths and vermin destroy, and where thieves break in and steal" (Matthew 6:19–21). For example, Dave's automobiles will wear out and depreciate while he is on earth. Further, the satisfaction he gets from his fancy cars and prestigious golf club is temporary and does not lead to heavenly treasures.

Likewise, Diane's accumulation of clothes and trinkets is also temporal. Sadly, the moment she passes from this life, she will realize these things hold no eternal value (1 Timothy 6:6–8).

QUESTION #2

Based on your answer to the first question, where is Dave and Diane's heart? What do they genuinely treasure? Before you write your response, recall Jesus's words, "For where your treasure is, there your heart will be also" (Matthew 6:21).

_____

_____

_____

_____

_____

_____

TOM'S COMMENT

Dave and Diane are more concerned about their material possessions than things of eternal value. For example, Dave places a high value on his expensive car and extravagant golf membership. At the same time, Diane enjoys spending money on non-essential items that are mainly wants and desires, not needs.

QUESTION #3

Suppose that Dave and Diane were open to financial counseling. What biblically-based financial advice would you offer them? Provide a Scripture reference for each point.

_____

_____

_____

_____

_____

_____

TOM'S COMMENT

Dave and Diane need to make a paradigm shift from focusing on material things to those of eternal value. In Colossians 3:1–2, Paul said, "Since, then, you have been raised with Christ, set your hearts on things above, where Christ is, seated at the right hand of God. Set your minds on things above, not on earthly things."

Dave and Diane must realize that they focus on material things—temporary "treasures on earth" that will be lost the moment they die. Ecclesiastes 5:15 states, "Everyone comes naked from their mother's womb, and as everyone comes, so they depart. They take nothing from their toil that they can carry in their hands."

Dave and Diane would be well advised to purchase a less expensive car and keep it for ten years instead of trading it every few years. In addition, Dave should cut back on what he spends on golfing, while Diane should reduce her spending at the shopping mall.

Dave and Diane need to learn contentment (Philippians 4:11–13), which would reduce their spending on wants and desires. This would result in a monthly surplus cash flow, allowing them to pay down debt and give more to God's work.

2. There Is Hope Because It's Never Too Late to Change

If you have mismanaged God's resources and stored up more treasures on earth than in heaven, be encouraged that it is never too late to change your focus! Above all else, never forget the words of 1 John 1:9: "If we confess our sins, he is faithful and just and will forgive us our sins and purify us from all unrighteousness." Further, the Lord is compassionate toward us and knows our weaknesses. Note Hebrews 4:15–16:

> "We do not have a high priest who is unable to empathize with our weaknesses, but we have one who has been tempted in every way, just as we are—yet he did not sin. Let us then approach God's throne of grace with confidence, so that we may receive mercy and find grace in our time of need."

In other words, if you repent of mismanaging your money, material things, time, and talents, and ask the Lord to forgive you, He will! However, from now on, it is essential you fulfill your stewardship responsibilities in these areas according to God's word and biblical principles.

To help you gain an eternal perspective and the resulting rewards in heaven, I recommend you study and meditate on God's word (Joshua 1:8) concerning finances to allow God to change how you think about and manage money and material things. Further, you can follow Paul's counsel in Colossians 3:1–2:

> "Since, then, you have been raised with Christ, set your hearts on things above, where Christ is, seated at the right hand of God. Set your minds on things above, not on earthly things."

If your heart and mind are truly set on things above, God will bless you while you are on earth and, more significantly, forever in heaven!

3. Summary of Store Up Treasures in Heaven, Not on Earth

Most Christians need to make a paradigm shift by changing their focus from temporal things and pleasures—treasures on earth to things that will last for eternity—treasures in heaven.

Treasures in heaven include developing a close personal relationship with Jesus Christ, giving generously to God's work, sharing the gospel, serving the Lord in ministry, possessing a genuine faith and godly character, and being an effective witness for the Lord (2 Peter 1:5–11).

To follow the Lord faithfully, many Christians will need to surrender some earthly treasures. However, from an eternal perspective, their lives will be more fulfilling and effective for God's kingdom. This will result in the Lord blessing them and others abundantly while on earth and in heaven.

VI.

HOW YOU MANAGE MONEY IMPACTS ETERNITY

A. KEY BIBLICAL QUESTION

The following question is one that most Christians do not adequately consider or address thoroughly enough:

"Does the way you manage money and material possessions on earth impact eternity in a significant way?"

According to Scripture, the answer is a resounding yes—and far more than we think!

For example, suppose you acknowledge in your heart and mind that you are a steward of God's resources (Haggai 2:8); you learn and apply biblical financial principles, like developing and implementing a budget (Luke 14:28–30); you choose to be content with less (1 Timothy 6:6–8); and you give generously to God's work (2 Corinthians 9:6–11). If you do, then, we are assured that these things will positively impact eternity. Why?

The reason is that each of these principles is based on God's word, and we know that God's word will not come back void but will accomplish all He desires. Note Isaiah 55:11, which says, "my word that goes out from my mouth ... will not return to me empty, but will accomplish what I desire and achieve the purpose for which I sent it."

In other words, when others see your "good works," particularly your godly stewardship of God's resources, they will see Christ in you, and as such, they may come to know Jesus as their personal Saviour. Therefore, how you live and how you give is an evangelistic message that leads others to Christ and impacts their souls both now and in eternity.

When you reach heaven, I am confident there will be individuals in glory who would not have made it there without your generous gifts of money, material items, or the time you spent helping to advance the gospel.

Your contributions to various ministries, like your church, radio, television, Christian camps, youth outreaches, and so forth, may have touched their lives. These souls will likely thank you for such things, which resulted in their hearing the message of salvation and inheriting eternal life.

An individual's salvation is of utmost importance to God, so it must also be for us who follow Him. We must never forget that a person's salvation is for eternity, and the rewards, or lack of rewards we receive in heaven for our faithful management of God's resources, including our time and money, are also for eternity (Matthew 16:27).

With that in mind, let's suppose you spend your earthly resources, including your time and money, on your personal wants and desires instead of investing them into God's kingdom. In that case, it is possible that those in your circle of influence would not come to know Christ as their Saviour or be discipled due to your lack of faithfulness, and the positive impact you could have made on eternity will be lost.

1. Our Lives on Earth Compared to Eternity

Think about this, most people live between 60 and 90 years, while few will survive beyond 100 years. Thus, our life on earth is brief compared to the time we will spend in eternity.

How long do you think you will be in heaven? Thirty million years? Perhaps thirty billion years? The sobering truth is that your time in heaven will be forever, since heaven is a place without end!

Consider the following Scripture verses concerning our lives on earth:

"What is your life? You are a mist that appears for a little while and then vanishes" (James 4:14).

"Teach us to number our days, that we may gain a heart of wisdom" (Psalm 90:12).

"Show me, LORD, my life's end and the number of my days; let me know how fleeting my life is. You have made my days a mere handbreadth; the span of my years is as nothing before you. Everyone is but a breath" (Psalm 39:4–5).

As these verses attest, our time on earth is extremely short. Therefore, how we utilize the resources, such as our money, time, gifts, and talents, that God entrusted to us while on earth will significantly impact eternity.

Consequently, our faithful stewardship of all our resources, including giving generously to God's work, will result in lasting rewards in heaven that you and other followers of Christ will enjoy for eternity!

2. God Will Judge Fairly as He Is "All-Knowing" and "Present Everywhere"

God's word clearly states that the Lord will judge everyone (Acts 17:31) and that He will judge fairly (Genesis 18:25). Jeremiah 17:10 says, "I the LORD search the heart and examine the mind, to reward each person according to their conduct, according to what their deeds deserve."

Furthermore, the Lord will examine our motives and provide rewards or lack of rewards in proportion to our works on while on earth. As stated in 1 Corinthians 4:5:

> "Judge nothing before the appointed time; wait until the Lord comes. He will bring to light what is hidden in darkness and will expose the motives of the heart. At that time each will receive their praise from God" (emphasis added).

Many Christians need to realize that the rewards they will receive in heaven will benefit them and others for all eternity! As a result, we should wisely invest the money, time, and talents God has given us into His kingdom work so that we can "store up treasures in heaven." As a result, we will enjoy those rewards and treasures forever. God is good!

Unfortunately, most Christians focus on temporal things, such as worldly wants and desires that will be forever lost when they die. The apostle Paul reminds us in 1 Timothy 6:7, "For we brought nothing into the world, and we can take nothing out of it."

3. Warning: The Judgment of God Awaits Everyone

The Bible refers to two eternal judgments: one for believers and one for unbelievers.

All true believers will pass the "judgment of faith" in Christ because they have accepted Jesus as their Saviour and Lord; thus they are forgiven of their sins. But on the other hand, all unbelievers will fail the "judgment of faith" at the "great white throne judgment" since their names will not be written in the "Book of Life" (Revelation 20:11–15). Further, in John 5:28–29, Jesus said:

> "Do not be amazed at this, for a time is coming when all who are in their graves will hear his voice and come out— those who have done good will rise to live, and those who have done what is evil will rise to be condemned."

However, when Christians reach heaven, their faith is not the only thing that will be judged. They will also be judged for their works. Regarding God's future judgment of His people, Proverbs 24:12 states, "Will he not repay each one according to what they have done?" And note 2 Corinthians 5:10, which states: "We must all appear before the *judgment seat of Christ*, so that each of us may receive what is due us for the things done while in the body, whether good or bad" (emphasis added).

4. The Judgment Seat of Christ

At the judgment seat of Christ, Christians will be given rewards or lack of rewards (Matthew 19:27; 1 Corinthians 3:12–15) and varying levels of responsibility and authority while they are in heaven (see the parable of the ten minas in Luke 19:11–26, which I will cover in more detail in chapter VII).

5. All Are Held Individually Accountable

In Romans 14:12, the apostle Paul said, "Each of us will give an account of ourselves to God." Further, 1 Peter 4:5 says, "They will have to give account to him who is ready to judge the living and the dead."

In this Scripture, "the living" refers to those who are spiritually alive in Christ because they have accepted Jesus as their Saviour and Lord, while "the dead" refers to those who are spiritually dead since they have never accepted Jesus as their Saviour and Lord.

God will judge both the living and the dead but in different ways. Christians will appear before the judgment seat of Christ (the bema) to receive rewards or lack thereof for their works and service to God (2 Corinthians 5:10). They will not be condemned (Romans 8:1) but rather forgiven of their sins and destined to spend eternity with Christ.

Unbelievers who are spiritually dead and have not put their faith in Jesus Christ will be judged and punished according to their actions during their earthly lives. The more severe their offence, the more severe their punishment. There will be no defence and no appeal for the unbeliever.

Remember, God will bring every deed into judgment. In Ecclesiastes 12:13–14, Solomon said:

"Now all has been heard; here is the conclusion of the matter: Fear God and keep his commandments, for this is the duty of all mankind. For God will bring every deed into judgment, including every hidden thing, whether it is good or evil."

6. Jesus Is Preparing a Place for Us in Heaven

Many Christians focus on finding the perfect house or renovating their home. While there is nothing wrong with having a lovely home, our time on earth is very brief compared to eternity. For this reason, a wise Christian invests in God's kingdom to enjoy an even greater home in heaven for all eternity!

For Christians, our true home is in heaven, not on earth. As Paul stated in 2 Corinthians 5:6–8, "We are always confident and know that as long as we are at home in the body we are away from the Lord ... and would prefer to be away from the body and at home with the Lord."

According to God's word, many great men and women of faith continued to live by faith until their death. Note excerpts from Hebrews 11:13, 16:

"All these people were still living by faith when they died ... admitting that they were foreigners and strangers on earth ... longing for a better country—a heavenly one. Therefore God is not ashamed to be called their God, for he has prepared a city for them."

As followers of Christ, we are also "foreigners and strangers on earth" who should be longing for a better destination—a heavenly one, instead of desiring the things of this world. Therefore, this is where our focus must be. In this way, God will never be ashamed to be called our God as He prepares an eternal place for us.

And indeed, in John 14:2–3, Jesus promised that He is going to prepare a place for us:

> "My Father's house has many rooms; if that were not so, would I have told you that I am going there to prepare a place for you? And if I go and prepare a place for you, I will come back and take you to be with me that you also may be where I am."

Therefore, we need to understand that when we use our money, time, and talents to accumulate things on earth to satisfy our selfish wants and desires, they do not and cannot produce anything of lasting value because they are temporary. *However, money and material things can be converted into things of eternal value if they're given and used for God's work to spread the gospel, disciple believers, and help the poor!*

7. There Will Be Rewards for Managing Money and Resources God's Way

The following Scriptures illustrate how faithful stewardship of God's money and resources will be rewarded.

- In Matthew 19:29, Jesus said that believers who give generously and sacrifice much in their earthly lives "will receive a hundredfold" in eternity (ESV).

- God will not overlook our good works! Ephesians 6:8 says, "You know that the Lord will reward each one for whatever good they do."

- God promises great rewards for all who faithfully serve Him (Revelation 11:18).

God rewards those who give to the poor. Matthew 19:21 says, "Go, sell your possessions and give to the poor, and you will have treasure in heaven."

- Those who help others *without expecting anything in return* will be rewarded. In Luke 14:13–14, Jesus said, "When you give a banquet, invite the poor, the crippled, the lame, the blind, and you will be blessed. Although they cannot repay you, you will be repaid at the resurrection of the righteous."

- Those who trust God amid difficult trials and persevere under persecution will reap great rewards (Hebrews 10:34–36).

- In Luke 6:22–23, Jesus said: "Blessed are you when people hate you, when they exclude you and insult you and reject your name as evil, because of the Son of Man. Rejoice in that day and leap for joy, because great is your reward in heaven."

- God will richly reward Christians who live a holy and blameless life (1 Peter 3:11–14).

8. The Reward of Rulership and Authority

During the millennial reign of Christ, believers will "reign and rule" with the Lord over the earth and its inhabitants (see Revelation 20). God's word indicates that those who have proved to be faithful servants will be put "in charge of many things" (Matthew 25:20–23), while some will "rule over cities" (Luke 19:17, 19 NCV).

The level of responsibility and authority rewarded to a believer will be proportionate to their faithfulness or lack thereof in managing the money and resources entrusted to them during their earthly lives (see the parable of the ten minas in Luke 19:17–26).

Revelation 2:26–27 says, "To the one who is victorious and does my will to the end, I will given authority over the nations… just as I have received authority from my Father."

To summarize, all genuine followers of Jesus Christ will be with the Lord in heaven. However, the Lord will assign varying degrees of responsibility and authority to each *depending on their level of faithful stewardship while on earth.*

9. The Five Crown Rewards in Heaven

As well as eternal rewards, the New Testament speaks of five crowns to be rewarded in heaven—again, depending on how followers of Jesus Christ managed the money, time, and talents entrusted to them while on earth.

10. Crown #1: The Crown of Life

The "crown of life" will be rewarded to believers who maintain their commitment to Christ during times of persecution. James 1:12 says:

"Blessed is the one who perseveres under trial because, having stood the test, that person will receive the crown of life that the Lord has promised to those who love him."

Further, Revelation 2:10 says, "Be faithful, even to the point of death, and I will give you life as your victor's crown."

11. Crown #2: The Incorruptible Crown

The "incorruptible crown" will be rewarded to believers for their self-discipline, determination, and victory in the Christian life, which includes managing one's earthly money and resources God's way.

First Corinthians 9:24–25 states:

"Do you not know that in a race all the runners run, but only one gets the prize? Run in such a way as to get the prize. Everyone who competes in the games goes into strict training. They do it to get a crown that will not last, but we do it to get a crown that will last forever."

This is one of my favourite Scriptures! Note that when Christians manage money God's way and intentionally store up treasures in heaven rather than treasures on earth, God will reward them with a crown that will last forever!

12. Crown #3: The Crown of Rejoicing

The "crown of rejoicing" will be rewarded to those who pour themselves out to bring others to Christ through evangelism and discipleship. First Thessalonians 2:19 says, "What is our hope, our joy, or the crown in which we will glory in the presence of our Lord Jesus when he comes? Is it not you?"

And in Philippians 4:1, Paul addresses his beloved converts, "My brothers and sisters, you whom I love and long for, my joy and crown, stand firm in the Lord in this way."

13. Crown #4: The Crown of Righteousness

The "crown of righteousness" will be rewarded to those who joyfully purify and ready themselves to meet their Saviour and Lord at His return. These believers are not caught up with earthly matters; rather, they long for heaven, their true home. Note 2 Timothy 4:7–8, where Paul says:

> "I have fought the good fight, I have finished the race, I have kept the faith. Now there is in store for me the crown of righteousness, which the Lord, the righteous Judge, will award to me on that day—and not only to me, but also to all who have longed for his appearing."

14. Crown #5: The Crown of Glory

The "crown of glory" will be rewarded to those believers who faithfully represent Christ in positions of spiritual leadership. First Peter 5:2–4 says:

> "Be shepherds of God's flock that is under your care, watching over them—not because you must, but because you are willing, as God wants you to be; not pursuing dishonest gain, but eager to serve; not lording it over those entrusted to you, but being examples to the flock. And when the Chief Shepherd appears, you will receive the crown of glory that will never fade away."

Recall that in 1 Timothy 3:3–4, an elder is required to be, among other things, "not a lover of money" and one who "manages his own family well." Certainly, managing one's family well includes godly financial management. Christian leaders who mismanage their finances and resources on earth may lose the reward of the crown of glory in heaven.

It would be ideal if more church leaders understood this, since many fail to follow God's biblical principles when managing personal or church finances. In most cases, this is due to the spiritual leaders not understanding God's word concerning money, except for tithing.

15. Summary of Crowns in Heaven

In summary, these crowns will be an eternal blessing for the believer that will never fade away. But, most significantly, they will bring glory to Christ Jesus as we lay them before His feet (Revelation 4:10). We will cast our crowns before the Lord in recognition of having lived a godly life, but most importantly, to praise God as all the honor and glory belongs to Him!

Although every Christian should seek these rewards, no crown will ever compare to the splendour of meeting God face to face. Until that day, we need to live a life that ultimately pleases our Lord, including how we manage the money and resources He has entrusted to us on this side of eternity.

16. Eternal Differences in Heaven

There are varying levels of rewards for Christians in heaven based on their faithfulness to God on earth. For example, not every Christian will hear the words, "Well done, good and faithful servant!" (Matthew 25:23), and not all believers will have "treasures in heaven" (Matthew 6:19–21).

Furthermore, not all believers will be given the same degree of responsibility or position of authority in heaven (Luke 19:17, 26). In Matthew 16:27, Jesus said, "The Son of Man is going to come in his Father's glory with his angels, and then he will reward each person according to what they have done."

In essence, Christians will receive different levels of rewards in heaven based on how well they managed the money, material resources, time, and talents God gave them during their earthly life.

17. God is All-Knowing and Cannot Be Fooled

We know from the Scriptures that God has perfect knowledge and understanding of absolutely everything. He does not need to learn anything, nor does He forget anything! In Hebrews 4:13, Paul says, "Nothing in all creation is hidden from God's sight. Everything is uncovered and laid bare before the eyes of him to whom we must give account."

First Corinthians 4:5 states:

"Judge nothing before the appointed time; wait until the Lord comes. He will bring to light what is hidden in darkness and will expose the motives of the heart. At that time each will receive their praise from God."

Again, if someone accepts Jesus Christ as their Saviour and Lord, their sins are forgiven, and they will spend eternity in heaven with the Lord. However, their rewards, or lack thereof, will be based on their stewardship of the money, material things, time, and talents God provided them during their earthly lives.

Sadly, in my experience, most Christians fail to appreciate that how they utilize their money, material resources, time, and talents for the Lord while on earth will affect their rewards and crowns in heaven for all eternity.

18. Be Motivated to Give to God's Work for Eternal Reasons

Christians must give to the Lord and serve Him with godly motives. Proverbs 16:2 says, "All a person's ways seem pure to them, but motives are weighed by the LORD." Therefore, if you do something with selfish motives, including giving to God's work, God will not reward you (Matthew 6:1–4).

The apostle Paul encouraged all believers to be motivated by *eternal rewards* (Galatians 6:9–10). Note Paul's words in 1 Timothy 6:17–19:

"Command those who are rich in this present world not to be arrogant nor to put their hope in wealth, which is so uncertain, but to put their hope in God, who richly provides us with everything for our enjoyment. Command them to do good, to be rich in good deeds, and to be generous and willing to share. In this way they will lay up treasure for themselves as a firm foundation for the coming age, so that they may take hold of the life that is truly life."

And of course, managing money and resources God's way must be motivated primarily by our genuine love for Christ and our gratitude for what He has accomplished for us on the cross so we could have eternal life in the first place.

In Hebrews 11:26, Moses "regarded disgrace for the sake of Christ as of greater value than the treasures of Egypt, because he was looking ahead to his reward." Likewise, as Christians we need to have an eternal perspective and work diligently while on earth to maximize our treasures in heaven, as instructed by Jesus in Matthew 6:19–21.

19. The Parable of the Shrewd (Dishonest) Manager

In Luke 16, Jesus told a parable about a manager who wasted his master's possessions. So the master called him up on it and told him to give an account of his management because he could no longer be the manager.

Before his termination, the manager goes to his master's debtors and reduces their debts, thereby gaining their friendship. When the master learns of this, he praises the steward for his foresight in making friends with those who could support him after his employment ceases. While the master disapproved of his manager's dishonesty, he was impressed with his manager's foresight in accessing the resources he wanted to meet his future needs.

This nonbelieving steward's time horizon was strictly his time on earth. Clearly, he had no vision for eternity in heaven, so being dishonest would not be an issue for him—he was just interested in meeting his needs after he lost his job. On the other hand, a Christian's time horizon includes eternity in heaven, so wise Christians must invest money in such a way that they will "be welcomed into eternal dwellings" (Luke 16:9).

One of the fundamental principles of the parable of the shrewd (dishonest) manager is that nonbelievers are often shrewder than believers when considering their time horizon, which is solely their life on earth. Meanwhile, 99.999 per cent of a Christian's life will be spent in heaven for eternity. Therefore, Christians need to utilize their money, material things, spiritual gifts, and natural abilities for eternal purposes, including investing their resources into God's work.

20. Questions to Consider About Handling True Riches

In Luke 16:11, Jesus said, "If you have not been trustworthy in handling worldly wealth, who will trust you with true riches?"

QUESTION #1

What are the true riches Jesus referred to?

_____

_____

_____

TOM'S COMMENT

"True riches" can mean several things, but I would include the following:

- Having a close relationship with the Lord Jesus Christ.

- Being involved in an effective ministry for God's kingdom.

- Participating in evangelism and the salvation of souls.

- Giving money to God's work with godly motives, resulting in heavenly rewards (Matthew 19:29; 6:19–21).

229

In Luke 16:11, Jesus asserts that if someone cannot be trusted with something of lesser importance, such as money, which is temporal, then why would God trust them with something of much greater importance, such as one of the true riches listed above?

In light of this, it makes sense for every Christian to ensure they manage their money according to God's principles and specific will and give generously to God's work to experience God's true, eternal riches.

B. CASE STUDY, QUESTIONS, TOM'S COMMENTS

1. Case Study: A Couple Renovate Their Home

Enrique and Sofia are a married couple who are sincere Christians. They take an active role in their church and faithfully tithe around 10 per cent of their combined incomes regularly. Both earn above-average salaries, so they are well off financially.

The couple are blessed with a beautiful home that is in excellent condition. Nevertheless, they decide to update and renovate most of their house. Their savings are sufficient to pay for the renovations without going into debt, and they believe they are entitled to enjoy the wealth God has provided them.

However, as with most renovations, the total cost was significantly higher than their initial estimate. The increased expense came from their decision to make more significant improvements than initially planned. Also, because of the large amount of money they spent, both felt concerned they might not recover their investment should they ever sell their home. Even so, they have an even lovelier place to enjoy for the foreseeable future, which makes them happy.

Meanwhile, out of concern, a Christian friend asks Enrique and Sofia if their renovations are necessary. The couple justifies their spending by saying they need a much nicer house than most because they plan to host a home-based Bible study for their church.

QUESTION #1

Will Enrique and Sofia's home renovation expenditures result in "treasures in heaven" or "treasures on earth"?

_____

_____

_____

_____

_____

_____

TOM'S COMMENT

The truth is that Enrique and Sofia's investment is mostly if not entirely, a "treasure on earth" since it is not a direct investment in God's kingdom—like a church, Christian ministry, or an outreach that disciples others or leads people to Christ.

Further, their extensive home renovations were not required for them to host a Bible study in their home, which was how they rationalized their extravagant spending. Enrique and Sofia likely made this investment solely for their personal pleasure. Thus, it is reasonable to conclude that God would consider this renovation a "treasure on earth" rather than a "treasure in heaven."

QUESTION #2

In John 14:2–3, Jesus said, "In my Father's house are many mansions: if it were not so, I would have told you. I go to prepare a place for you. And if I go and prepare a place for you, I will come again, and receive you unto myself; that where I am, there ye may be also" (KJV). In that context, do you think it is more profitable to invest in "treasures on earth" or "treasures in heaven"?

_____

_____

_____

_____

TOM'S COMMENT

In many places in Scripture, God promises rewards to Christians (Matthew 16:27) who willingly sacrifice and invest in things of eternal value, such as ministries that focus on evangelism and discipleship. In addition, God blesses those who give to the poor. Matthew 19:21 says, "Go, sell your possessions and give to the poor, and you will have treasure in heaven."

QUESTION #3

In light of the above Scriptures, what are more fruitful ways Enrique and Sofia could have invested their significant surplus of funds?

_____

_____

_____

_____

TOM'S COMMENT

It is not necessarily wrong or unbiblical for a Christian to renovate their home. And in some cases, the Lord may even direct an individual or couple to undertake a renovation project.

However, in many cases, Christians spend considerable money fixing up their earthly homes. Yet, if they invested those funds into the Lord's work, they would receive an even greater home in heaven, like a mansion (John 14:2), that they could enjoy forever!

I am not suggesting that Christians should live in poverty, but it is so important to understand that when we stand before the Lord at the judgment seat of Christ (2 Corinthians 5:10), our works will be tested by fire, as Paul describes in 1 Corinthians 3:13–15:

> "Their work will be shown for what it is, because the Day will bring it to light. It will be revealed with fire, and the fire will test the quality of each person's work. If what has been built survives, the builder will receive a reward. If it is burned up, the builder will suffer loss but yet will be saved—even though only as one escaping through the flames."

There are numerous material things and pleasures followers of Christ spend their money on, which will "be burned up" at the judgment seat of Christ and result in no heavenly rewards.

Therefore, wise Christians who live with an eternal perspective will use the money, time, and talents God entrusts to them while on earth to make an eternal and lasting difference for others, especially those who receive Jesus as their Saviour and Lord.

2. Highlights of Key Biblical Principles of How You Manage Money Impacts Eternity

The following are the main highlights of this chapter's content:

1. How we handle God's money and resources *now* will have an enormous and lasting impact on our lives in eternity.

2. There will be significant rewards in heaven for the faithful steward. However, those who selfishly spend their money and resources on their personal wants and desires will receive few rewards.

3. Biblical warnings about the coming judgment are clear, although judgment will differ for believers and nonbelievers. Specifically, God will judge Christians at the judgment seat of Christ (bema) based on how they used the money and resources He entrusted to them (2 Corinthians 5:10), which I will expand on in the next chapter.

4. Every person will be held accountable to God (1 Corinthians 4:5). Therefore, it doesn't matter how many Christians you know who are terrible stewards of their money and resources, like spending on their selfish desires and not tithing or giving little to God's work. The choices others make are irrelevant, as God will judge you and me individually. In Romans 14:12, the apostle Paul said, "Each of us will give an account of ourselves to God."

5. God's word says we will reap what we sow. Note Galatians 6:7–9:

"Do not be deceived: God cannot be mocked. A man reaps what he sows. Whoever sows to please their flesh, from the flesh will reap destruction; whoever sows to please the Spirit, from the Spirit will reap eternal life. Let us not become weary in doing good, for at the proper time we will reap a harvest if we do not give up."

6. We must never forget that God owns everything (Haggai 2:8). Thus, we are merely stewards of God's money, which we should manage according to God's principles (2 Timothy 3:16–17) and God's specific will (Psalm 32:8).

7. Even if you are a high-income earner and you've worked hard for your money, you cannot claim credit for your success. Note Deuteronomy 8:17–18, which says:

"You may say to yourself, 'My power and the strength of my hands have produced this wealth for me.' But remember the LORD your God, for it is he who gives you the ability to produce wealth."

3. Summary of How You Manage Money Impacts Eternity

In light of the eternal rewards you will receive in heaven and tremendous benefits to be enjoyed by many and yourself for eternity, it makes perfect sense to use your money, time, talents, and giftings for eternal purposes.

In the words of Randy Alcorn and R.G. LeTourneau, "You can't take it with you, but you can send it on ahead." Further, a well-known missionary, Jim Elliot, once said, "He is no fool who gives up what he cannot keep to gain what he cannot lose."

Moreover, the apostle Paul wrote in Colossians 3:1–2:

"Since, then, you have been raised with Christ, set your hearts and things above, where Christ is, seated at the right hand of God. Set your minds on things above, not on earthly things."

In other words, focus on things that have lasting value as you *keep your eyes on eternity.* And remember my perspective: *Investing your money and resources into God's work is a practical and biblical way to convert temporal assets into eternal benefits!*

VII.

THE JUDGMENT SEAT OF CHRIST AND THE GREAT WHITE THRONE JUDGMENT

A. KEY BIBLICAL PRINCIPLE

Jesus Christ will judge all genuine Christians at the "judgment seat of Christ" (also known as the bema). We will receive rewards or lack of rewards, depending on how we used the resources God entrusted to us while we were on earth.

1. What Is the "Bema"?

In the Bible, the term "bema" is taken from the Greek word for judgment. The "bema" seat refers to a raised platform on which a judge sits, resembling a throne. It is another title given to the judgment seat of Christ.

Note 2 Corinthians 5:10, "We must all appear before the judgment seat of Christ, so that each of us may receive what is due us for the things done while in the body, whether good or bad."

It's important to understand that, as with all Christians, you will stand before Jesus Christ at the judgment seat of Christ to receive rewards or lack of rewards, as well as different levels of authority in heaven for the things you did, whether good or bad, while living on earth (see Luke 19:11–26).

Those who genuinely trust in Jesus Christ as their personal Saviour and Lord will be forgiven of their sins, as Christ paid the penalty for all our sins at the cross. Every true believer will spend eternity in heaven because of His gift of salvation (John 3:16; Ephesians 2:8–9). Praise be to God!

However, the rewards God distributes at the judgment seat of Christ will vary from person to person. For example, Christians who work hard while on earth and use their money, time, and talents to bring glory to God will receive great rewards in heaven for all eternity.

On the other hand, those who have not been good stewards of God's resources will "suffer loss" of rewards in heaven (1 Corinthians 3:15). Paul addressed believers specifically in 1 Corinthians 3:11–15:

> "No one can lay any foundation other than the one already laid, which is Jesus Christ. If anyone builds on this foundation using gold, silver, costly stones, wood, hay or straw, their work will be shown for what it is, because the Day [the judgment seat of Christ] will bring it to light. It will be revealed with fire, and the fire [God's fire] will test the quality of each person's work. If what has been built survives, the builder will receive a reward. If it is burned up, the builder will suffer loss but yet will be saved—even though only as one escaping through the flames."

In other words, our works are defined by what we do with God's resources, such as our money, possessions, time, natural abilities, and spiritual gifts that God has entrusted to us while we are here on earth. "God's fire" will reveal the quality of these works and the eternal significance of what we did with our resources while on earth.

According to the above passage, those works represented by gold, silver, and precious stones will be purified by fire and benefit us for eternity in heaven! However, those works represented by wood, hay, or straw will be burnt up and not rewarded.

2. Works That Produce Eternal Benefits

Some of the works that will result in rewards in heaven are as follows:

- Participating in activities that result in the salvation of others, such as giving your time and resources to a local church, evangelical Christian organization, or outreach.

- Witnessing to others will result in rewards in heaven because God values an individual's salvation above all else.

- Giving generously to God's work will undoubtedly be rewarded in heaven (Matthew 16:27; 19:29).

- Laboring as "working for the Lord" with the right motive in your heart. Colossians 3:23–24 says, "Whatever you do, work at it with all your heart, as working for the Lord, not for human masters, since you know you will receive an inheritance from the Lord as a reward. It is the Lord Christ you are serving." Proverbs 16:2 says, "All a person's ways seem pure to them, but motives are weighed by the Lord." Therefore, works rooted in pure, godly motives will be rewarded, while everything else will burn up.

- Faithfully serving the Lord wherever He calls you to minister—in your church, parachurch organization,

239

or informally among your family, friends, neighbours, co-workers, and others (Ephesians 2:10).

- Giving to God's work confidentially. Recall Matthew 6 when the Pharisees announced their giving with trumpets to receive honor from men. But Jesus said in Matthew 6:1, "Be careful not to practice your righteousness in front of others to be seen by them. If you do, you will have no reward from your Father in heaven."

    Therefore, if you give to God's work in secret, without boasting or using money to manipulate others, there will be rewards for you in heaven.

Since Christians will stand before God at the judgment seat of Christ, the wise Christian will heed the instructions in Hebrews 12:1:

"Since we are surrounded by such a great cloud of witnesses, let us throw off everything that hinders and the sin that so easily entangles, and let us run with perseverance the race marked out for us."

3. Determine God's Calling for Your Life and Fulfil It

As you utilize the money and resources God has entrusted to you according to His biblical principles and specific will, you must also determine and fulfill God's calling on your life. Romans 11:29 says, "God's gifts and his call are irrevocable." Further, Ephesians 2:10 (ESV) states, "For we are [God's] workmanship, created in Christ Jesus for good works, which God prepared beforehand, that we should walk in them."

In other words, every child of God has a unique purpose to fulfil during their earthly life. Therefore, Christians who discern and accomplish God's calling for their lives will receive significant rewards in heaven.

Remember, God is for us and not against us (Romans 8:31). While all Christians are forgiven of their sins and destined to spend eternity in heaven (1 Thessalonians 4:17), different levels of rewards and authority in heaven will be given (see the parable of the ten minas in Luke 19). For those who have faithfully served Christ with their money, material resources, time, talents, and spiritual gifts, the judgment seat of Christ will be a joyful time of celebration!

B. QUESTIONS TO CONSIDER

QUESTION #1

What about those who have not been faithful stewards of God's resources?

_____

_____

_____

_____

_____

TOM'S COMMENT

Christians who have not utilized their money, material things, time, talents, and spiritual gifts for God's glory will suffer loss by having few rewards and crowns in heaven.

QUESTION #2

After we die, is it too late to store up treasures in heaven? (Matthew 6:19–21).

_____

_____

_____

_____

TOM'S COMMENT

The short answer is yes. Once we die, it's too late to change how we lived our earthly lives. No one will have a second opportunity to return to this earth to invest in God's kingdom to gain treasures in heaven. Therefore, a wise Christian understands that *now is the time to invest their money, time, gifts, and talents to store up treasures in heaven.*

Sadly, when many Christians reach heaven, I suspect they will wish they had given more generously to God's work, avoided unnecessary spending—especially on themselves—and invested more of their money and resources into Christian ministry, resulting in eternal benefits for themselves and others.

In light of this, I encourage you to study God's word on finances, apply biblical financial principles faithfully, and give sacrificially of your money, time, talents, and spiritual gifts for the work of the Lord. Then you can confidently trust God to reward you greatly in heaven for eternity!

You don't want to get to heaven and regret how you used your money and resources while you were on earth. Remember, money is temporary, and you will lose it all the second you die. Ecclesiastes 5:15 states,

"Everyone comes naked from their mother's womb, and as everyone comes, so they depart. They take nothing from their toil that they can carry in their hands."

Remember the words of Jim Elliot: "He is no fool who gives up what he cannot keep to gain what he cannot lose." The words of Randy Alcorn and R.G. Le Tourneau are also worth repeating: "You can't take it with you, but you can send it on ahead." This is particularly true regarding money! As I like to say, "Investing your money and resources into God's kingdom work is a practical and biblical way to convert a temporal asset into an eternal benefit!"

1. God Will Bring Every Deed into Judgment

Apart from Jesus Christ, Solomon was the wisest man who ever lived, as he wrote the Book of Proverbs and Ecclesiastes. Toward the end of his life, Solomon came to this wise conclusion:

"Now all has been heard; here is the conclusion of the matter: Fear God and keep his commandments, for this is the duty of all mankind. For God will bring every deed into judgment, including every hidden thing, whether it is good or evil" (Ecclesiastes 12:13–14).

2. What About Non-Christians?

Only those who have accepted Jesus Christ as their personal Saviour and Lord will appear before the judgment seat of Christ. Overall, it will be a joyous time as believers receive rewards for faithfully managing their money, time, talents, and spiritual gifts with a pure heart for God's glory and kingdom purposes.

However, unbelievers will not appear at the judgment seat of Christ. Instead, they will be required to attend the "great white throne judgment," as described in Revelation 20.

Though my words may seem harsh, I must speak the truth in love. According to God's word, the Bible, the sobering reality is that those who reject Jesus Christ as their Saviour and Lord will be judged accordingly. They will not have the protection and grace of the blood of Jesus Christ. Hence, they will be held accountable for their sins based on their own merits.

Note Hebrews 9:27: "People are destined to die once, and after that to face judgment." Further, 1 John 5:11–13 says:

> "This is the testimony: God has given us eternal life, and this life is in his Son. Whoever has the Son has life; whoever does not have the Son of God does not have life. I write these things to you who believe in the name of the Son of God so that you may know that you have eternal life."

In this passage, "life" refers to eternal life in heaven. As a result, non-Christians will not spend eternity in heaven with God because they rejected Jesus Christ as their Saviour and Lord. Consequently, their sins will not be forgiven. Rather, they will face eternal punishment at the great white throne judgment.

3. The Great White Throne Judgment

Revelation 20:11–15 describes the great white throne judgment to be faced by unbelievers as follows:

> "Then I saw a great white throne and him [Jesus Christ] who was seated on it. The earth and the heavens fled from

his presence, and there was no place for them. And I saw the dead, great and small, standing before the throne, and books were opened. Another book was opened, which is the book of life. The dead [*the spiritually dead who had no relationship with Jesus Christ*] were judged according to what they had done as recorded in the books. The sea gave up the dead that were in it, and death and Hades gave up the dead that were in them, and each person was judged according to what they had done. Then death and Hades were thrown into the lake of fire. The lake of fire is the second death. Anyone whose name was not found written in the book of life was thrown into the lake of fire" (emphasis added).

By nature, I am not a "fire and brimstone" speaker, but it's critical for people to know that if they reject Jesus Christ as their personal Saviour and Lord, they will spend eternity in the lake of fire, separated from God forever. I want to help you avoid that horrifying eternal consequence.

Second Peter 3:7 states, "By the same word the present heavens and earth are reserved for fire, being kept for the day of judgment and destruction of the ungodly."

The following chart summarizes the differences between the "judgment seat of Christ" and the "great white throne judgment."

4. Overview of the Similarities and Differences Between the Judgment Seat of Christ and the Great White Throne Judgment

THE JUDGMENT SEAT OF CHRIST	QUESTIONS FOR COMPARISON	THE GREAT WHITE THRONE JUDGMENT
Romans 14:10-12 1 Corinthians 3:10-4:5 2 Corinthians 5:1-10	What are Scripture references?	Revelation 20:11-15 Hebrews 9:27
Believers	Who will be judged?	Unbelievers
Jesus Christ	Who will be the judge?	Jesus Christ
To reward the faithful service of God's children	What is the purpose?	God's judgment of those who did not accept Jesus Christ
After the Rapture, during the Tribulation, before the Millennium	When will it occur?	After the Millennium, before the lake of fire

There will be no condemnation for true believers who will be forgiven for their sins (Romans 8:1). Faithful believers will receive rewards for their service to God	*What will be the criteria for judgment?*	Everyone who is spiritually dead, who has not put their faith in Jesus Christ, will be judged. There will be no defence and no appeal
Any good works done in the name of Jesus Christ will be rewarded (Matthew 16:27; 19:29)	*What will be the outcome?*	The spiritually dead will be cast into the lake of fire, eternally separated from God's presence
Each Christian's motives and reasons for serving God will be judged. Service for the Lord performed with pure and godly motives will be rewarded; all others will be burned (1 Corinthians 3:11-15; Proverbs 16:2)	*Will all those who are judged receive equal treatment? No.*	For the unbeliever, they will be condemned. The punishment will be worse for some than others depending upon what each person has done (Romans 2:5-9; Revelation 20:13)

All believers will receive credit for Jesus's righteousness, which delivers them from the punishment their sin deserves (Romans 3:23; 4:22-25; 6:23).	*Who will be punished for their sins?*	Because non-believers have rejected God's gift of salvation, they will receive the due punishment for their sins (John 3:18-20; Romans 1:18-23; 3:23)
Serve God with a pure heart and use the money, time, and talents God has entrusted to you for eternal purposes for His honor and glory.	*What should we do about it now?*	Repent of your sins, accept Jesus Christ as your Saviour and Lord (Mark 1:15), and serve God whole-heartedly. Do not wait! There may not be another chance (Matthew 24:36).

C. THE GOSPEL MESSAGE OF JESUS CHRIST

1. The Most Important Decision You Will Ever Make

If you have never accepted Jesus Christ as your personal Saviour and Lord, I urge you to seriously consider the following explanation of the gospel message.

2. First of All, God Loves You!

Jeremiah 31:3 says, "The LORD appeared to us in the past, saying: 'I have loved you with an everlasting love; I have drawn you with unfailing kindness.'" God wants to have a personal relationship with you that will last forever. In John 10:14–15, Jesus said, "I am the good shepherd; I know my sheep and my sheep know me— just as the Father knows me and I know the Father—and I lay down my life for the sheep."

3. Our Sin Separates Us from God

Romans 3:23 says, "All have sinned and fall short of the glory of God," and Romans 6:23 states, "The wages of sin is death, but the gift of God is eternal life in Christ Jesus our Lord."

And Isaiah 59:2 makes it clear: "Your iniquities have separated you from your God; your sins have hidden his face from you, so that he will not hear."

Please think about this diagram, which shows that sinful man is on one side and a sinless God is on the other side. A deep chasm separates sinful people and a holy God.

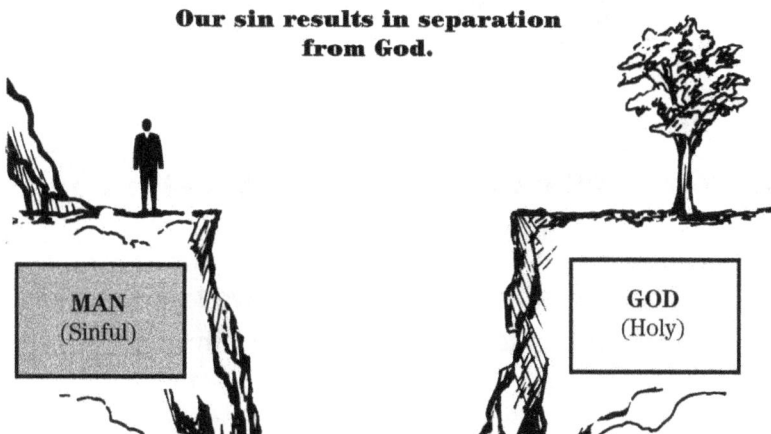

Our sin results in separation from God.

MAN (Sinful)

GOD (Holy)

4. Many Seek God the Wrong Way

It is written in Proverbs 14:12, "There is a way that appears to be right, but in the end it leads to death." Ephesians 2:8–9 clearly states that all people are entirely dependent on the Lord Jesus Christ for eternal salvation: "It is by grace you have been saved, through faith—and this is not from yourselves, it is the gift of God—not by works, so that no one can boast."

In other words, we cannot earn our way to heaven through good works, religion, philosophy, morality, or any other means.

None of our efforts can bridge this gap. There is only one remedy for this problem of separation from God...

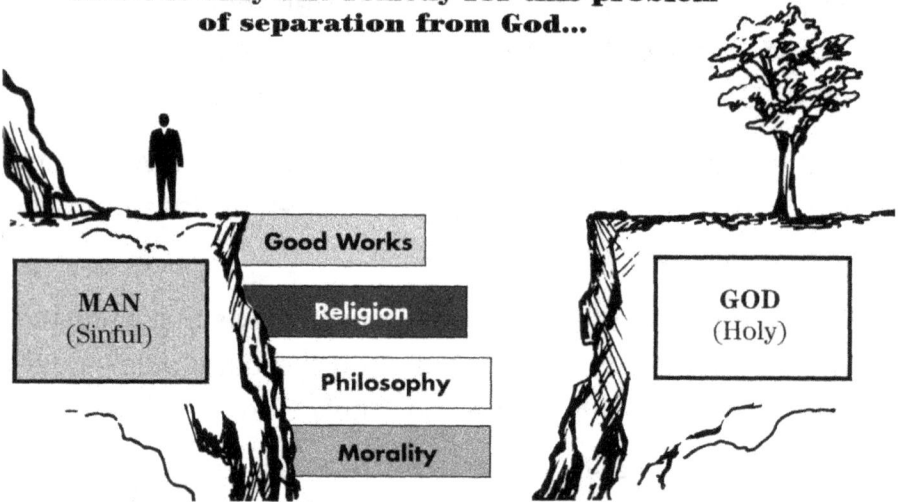

MAN (Sinful)

Good Works

Religion

Philosophy

Morality

GOD (Holy)

5. God Provides the Only Solution to Sin—His Son, Jesus Christ

In John 14:6, Jesus answered, "I am the way and the truth and the life. No one comes to the Father except through me."

The words of Romans 5:8 give us hope: "God demonstrates his own love for us in this: While we were still sinners, Christ died for us."

In other words, Jesus Christ provided the only solution by His death on the cross for the forgiveness of our sins.

**God has provided the only solution.
We must make the choice...**

6. Are You Willing to Do the Following?

1. The first step to reconciliation with God is to admit that you are a sinner who has sinned against God. Romans 3:23 tells us, "For all have sinned and fall short of the glory of God."

2. Considering this truth, you must turn away from your sins, follow God, and obey Him (Deuteronomy 28:1–12; Romans 10:9–10).

3. Believe that Jesus Christ died to forgive you of your sins; then open your heart to accept Him as your personal Saviour and Lord. John 3:16 says, "For God so loved the world that he gave his one and only Son, that whoever believes in him shall not perish but have eternal life."

4. Prayerfully call upon Jesus Christ to enter your heart and to take control of your life through the supernatural work of the Holy Spirit. In Revelation 3:20, Jesus provides you with this invitation when He says, "Here I am! I stand at the door and knock. If anyone hears my voice and opens the door, I will come in and eat with that person, and they with me." The "door" represents a person's heart.

Please understand that all I have done is cite some key Scriptures of the Bible. If you sense the desire to put your faith and trust in Jesus Christ, then the Holy Spirit of God is knocking at the door of your heart. Allow God's Spirit to enter your heart and give you His wisdom and guidance.

To accomplish this, I recommend you pray the following prayer to the Lord of the universe:

Dear Father God, I know I am a sinner and that I need Your forgiveness. I believe that Your Son, Jesus Christ, died for my sins. I am willing to turn from my sins. I now invite Jesus Christ to come into my heart and my life as my personal Saviour and Lord. I am willing, by God's strength, to follow and obey Jesus Christ as the Lord of my life.

7. If You Prayed This Prayer from Your Heart, Here Are Some of God's Promises

"Everyone who calls on the name of the Lord will be saved" (Romans 10:13). Saved from what? In 2 Thessalonians 1:8–9, God's position is clear:

> "He will punish those who do not know God and do not obey the gospel of our Lord Jesus. They will be punished with everlasting destruction and shut out from the presence of the Lord and from the glory of his might."

In other words, if you reject Jesus Christ as your Saviour and Lord, you will suffer eternal separation from God. The Bible refers to this as "hell," also known as "Hades" in Greek. Whatever name you ascribe to it, such a place is based on biblical truth. My intention is not to be unkind, but rather to tell you the truth for your eternal benefit. Therefore, I strongly encourage you to accept Jesus Christ as your personal Saviour and Lord today.

If you committed your life to the Lord, here's another promise from God, as stated in John 1:12–13:

> "To all who did receive him, to those who believed in his name, he gave the right to become children of God— children born not of natural descent, nor of human decision or a husband's will, but born of God."

If you sincerely prayed this prayer or a similar prayer, and accepted Jesus Christ as your personal Saviour and Lord, then you are a child of God. You are now privileged to enjoy a personal relationship with the Lord of the universe!

If this is the first time you've accepted Jesus Christ as your Saviour and Lord, visit to www.coplandfinancialministries.org, and send me an email so I can share some helpful literature with you and encourage you in your walk with the Lord!

8. Heavenly Rewards for Believers Who Serve the Lord Faithfully

God's word reminds us that we will give an account to God for how we lived our lives on earth and utilized the resources God entrusted to us. We will be rewarded accordingly. Note Romans 2:6–10:

> "God 'will repay each person according to what they have done.' To those who by persistence in doing good seek glory, honor and immortality, he will give eternal life. But for those who are self-seeking and who reject the truth and follow evil, there will be wrath and anger. There will be trouble and distress for every human being who does evil … but glory, honor and peace for everyone who does good."

In other words, Christians who use the money and resources entrusted to them by God according to His biblical principles and specific purpose, will be blessed and rewarded in heaven for eternity. However, those who reject Christ and follow after selfish gain will face God's eternal judgment.

9. Giving to Those Who Can Never Repay

In the parable of the great banquet, Jesus said:

"When you give a banquet, invite the poor, the crippled, the lame, the blind, and you will be blessed. Although they cannot repay you, you will be repaid at the resurrection of the righteous" (Luke 14:13–14).

And what is the result when believers give to the poor? *God will repay us when we are resurrected into heaven. To clarify, not only will God bless us in heaven when we give generously to His work, including helping the poor, but when we provide for our family's needs (not their wants and desires), God will bless us for that as well (1 Timothy 5:8; 1 Thessalonians 4:11–12).*

10. God Promises Crowns in Heaven for Faithful Believers

Although I covered this in the previous chapter, it is so important that it warrants repeating.

There are several crowns Christians can earn during their earthly lives and receive when they reach heaven. Here are some of them:

11. Crown #1: The Incorruptible Crown

In 1 Corinthians 9:24–25, Paul compared our life on earth to that of a race. Here's what he said:

"Do you not know that in a race all the runners run, but only one gets the prize? Run in such a way as to get the prize. Everyone who competes in the games goes into strict training. They do it to get a crown that will not last; but we do it to get a crown that will last forever."

12. Crown #2: The Crown of Righteousness

In 2 Timothy 4:7–8, the apostle Paul gives us a glimpse of his pilgrimage:

> "I have fought the good fight, I have finished the race, I have kept the faith. Now there is in store for me the crown of righteousness, which the Lord, the righteous Judge, will award to me on that day—and not only to me, but also to all who have longed for his appearing."

13. Crown #3: The Crown of Life

Many Christians will have to persevere under great trials, including financial trials. But when they do, God promises another crown in heaven! Note James 1:12, which says:

> "Blessed is the one who perseveres under trial because, having stood the test, that person will receive the crown of life that the Lord has promised to those who love him."

Ultimately, Christians who manage the money and resources entrusted to them according to God's biblical principles and specific will, including giving generously to God's work, will receive crowns in heaven for their faithfulness, perseverance, and righteousness.

In the case of Christians, we will all appear before the judgment seat of Christ after we die to give an account of our lives. In Romans 14:10, Paul asks, "You, then, why do you judge your brother or sister? Or why do you treat them with contempt? For we will all stand before God's judgment seat." He continues in verse 12, "Each of us will give an account of ourselves to God."

Being faithful to God in managing our money, time, talents, and spiritual gifts while on earth is essential to enjoying great rewards in heaven for eternity! First Corinthians 4:2 says, "Now it is required that those who have been given a trust must prove faithful."

14. Some Questions God Might Ask You When You Stand Before Jesus Christ on Judgment Day

Some questions the Lord Jesus might ask you when you reach heaven and stand before Him at the judgment seat of Christ are as follows:

- What did you do with the money and material things I entrusted to you? (1 Corinthians 4:2). Did you spend unnecessarily, perhaps on your selfish desires, or did you invest your money and resources into My work? Remember the basic stewardship principle that God owns everything, so we must manage money His way (Haggai 2:8; Psalm 24:1–2).

- Were your motives pure or selfish as you worked for Me, the Lord, including in your giving? Proverbs 16:2 states. "All a person's ways seem pure to them, but motives are weighed by the LORD."

- How did you spend the time I provided you on earth? Did you waste it on temporal things, or did you focus on things of eternal value, such as evangelism and discipleship of others? (Colossians 3:1–2).

- Did you utilize the natural talents and spiritual gifts I gave you to witness to other believers and disciple them?

As Paul spoke to believers in 1 Corinthians 3:11–15, he explained that at the judgment seat of Christ, God's fire will reveal the things we did that will result in eternal rewards, and the things we did that will burn and result in no eternal rewards. Ultimately, almighty God will judge our work for what it truly is.

God will give eternal rewards for good works, like giving generously, when done in the name of Jesus Christ with pure and godly motives. Therefore, to ensure your efforts will be rewarded by the Lord, commit to learning God's financial principles, and diligently apply them to manage the money and resources He has entrusted to you.

15. Additional Resources to Help You

There are many biblical financial principles and concepts I cannot cover entirely in this book. Please visit our ministry website at www.coplandfinancialministries.org where you can view a variety of videos related to finances at no cost.

In addition, you may order one of my other books:

1. *Financial Management God's Way*: This 12-week in-depth biblical-based financial study has helped many make the most profound and permanent changes in how they think about and manage money.

2. *Financial Moments, Biblical Principles that Will Transform How You Manage Money:* This book contains 360 of my "financial moments" currently aired on radio and television. It can be used as an excellent daily devotional, or to supplement your current devotions.

3. *Debt Reduction, Biblical Principles to Deal with Inflation, High Interest Rates, and Eliminating Debt:* At the time of writing, interest rates in Canada, the United States, and worldwide had increased substantially from March 2022 to March 2023, and inflation was a major concern. This book gives practical biblical advice on how to deal with high interest rates and the increased cost of living.

16. Chapter Summary—The Judgment Seat of Christ and the Great White Throne Judgment

The Bible clearly states that *Jesus Christ is the only way to inherit the gift of eternal life.* Sadly, those who choose *not to accept* Jesus Christ as their Saviour and Lord will be separated from God for all eternity and cast into the lake of fire.

I do not express my personal opinions or sentiments. Instead, I share the timeless truth of God's word out of care and concern for those who have not committed to a personal relationship with the Lord.

On the Day of Judgment, no one will be able to justify rejecting God's Son, Jesus Christ, as the word of God is perfectly clear. Therefore, I encourage you to consider the following Scriptures, which demonstrate that *only Jesus Christ can save a person's soul forever.*

17. Scripture Verses Revealing *Jesus Christ Is the Only Way to Eternal Life*

Jesus answered, "I am the way and the truth and the life. No one comes to the Father except through me" (John 14:6).

"For God so loved the world that he gave his one and only Son, that whoever believes in him shall not perish but have eternal life" (John 3:16).

"For there is one God and one mediator between God and mankind, the man Christ Jesus" (1 Timothy 2:5).

"There is a judge for the one who rejects me [Jesus Christ] and does not accept my words; the very words I have spoken will condemn them at the last day" (John 12:48).

"Whoever believes in the Son has eternal life, but whoever rejects the Son will not see life, for God's wrath remains on them" (John 3:36).

"For the wages of sin is death, but the gift of God is eternal life in Christ Jesus our Lord" (Romans 6:23).

"For the Son of Man [Jesus Christ] came to seek and to save the lost" (Luke 19:10).

I encourage you to *put your faith and trust in Jesus Christ today*. If our ministry team can help in any way, please contact us through our ministry website. You may also contact us by email: info@coplandfinancialministries.org.

18. Tom's Final Comments

Carefully consider that if you neglect to manage money and resources God's way, there may be relatively few rewards for you in heaven.

Once you leave this earth, you cannot return to relive your life. In other words, once you die, *there will be no second chance to "store up treasures in heaven"* (Matthew 6:19–21). Therefore:

- Be wise as you prioritize learning and applying God's biblical financial principles to your everyday life (Proverbs 12:15; Matthew 7:24).

- Make the paradigm shift to focus on things of eternal value instead of temporary things that have no lasting value. It is always worthwhile to spend time prayerfully seeking God's wisdom (James 1:5) and God's specific direction (Psalm 32:8) in utilizing the money and resources He has provided you.

- In all your endeavors, be sure to follow Jesus' instructions in Matthew 6:19–21:

  > "Do not store up for yourselves treasures on earth, where moths and vermin destroy, and where thieves break in and steal. But store up for yourselves treasures in heaven, where moths and vermin do not destroy, and where thieves do not break in and steal. For where your treasure is, there your heart will be also."

Finally, always remember that *investing your money and resources into God's work is a practical and biblical way to convert temporal assets into eternal benefits!*

FINANCIAL MOMENTS

WITH TOM COPLAND
(Chartered Professional Accountant)

*Biblical Principles that Will
Transform How You Manage Money*

CASTLE QUAY BOOKS

DEBT REDUCTION

WITH TOM COPLAND
(Chartered Professional Accountant)

Biblical Principles to Deal With Inflation, High Interest Rates, and Eliminating Debt

CASTLE QUAY BOOKS

www.ingramcontent.com/pod-product-compliance
Lightning Source LLC
Chambersburg PA
CBHW060300100426
42742CB00011B/1818